EMPOWERMENT OF DESTITUTE WOMEN THROUGH SWADHAR HOMES

EMPOWERMENT OF DESTITUTE WOMEN THROUGH SWADHAR HOMES

K.K. Srivastava

KALPAZ

ISBN : 978-93-5128-054-5
Price : ₹ 525

First Published, 2014

Published by

Kalpaz Publications
C-30, Satyawati Nagar,
Delhi-110052
Ph. : 9212142040
E-mail: kalpaz@hotmail.com

Laser Typesetting : Gyan Print (AB-II), Delhi
Printed at : G. Print Process, Delhi

Cataloging in Publication Data—DK
Courtesy: D.K. Agencies (P) Ltd. <docinfo@dkagencies.com>

Srivastava, K. K.
Empowerment of destitute women through Swadhar homes / K.K. Srivastava.
p. cm.
Includes bibliographical references (p.) and index.
ISBN 9789351280545

1. Women—India—Uttar Pradesh—Economic conditions. 2. Women—India—Karnataka—Economic conditions. 3. Women—India—Uttar Pradesh—Social conditions. 4. Women—India—Karnataka—Social conditions. 5. Women in development—Government policy—India—Uttar Pradesh. 6. Women in development—Government policy—India—Karnataka. 7. Women—Housing—India—Uttar Pradesh. 8. Women—Housing—India—Karnataka. 9. SvÁdhÁra (Organization). I. Title.

DDC 305.4209542 23

Dedicated to My
Babuji (Father)

Contents

Preface

Gender equality is an issue of primary importance to the welfare and progress of all nations. It is a fundamental requirement to achieve people-centred developments. What humanity needs is a world that is free, fair and equal; a world that will have no discrimination, violence or exploitation, a world where opportunity and prosperity are shared by all. Because discrimination begins in the minds of people, where gender bias becomes a habit in thought and action.

Women's empowerment is just a word in today's context. Women have come a long way today, and are actively participating in all walks of life – be it education, employment or politics. The National Commission for Women has achieved a lot towards the advancement of women's rights. Development of women has been receiving alternation of the government right from the First Five Year Plan to Eleventh Five Year Plan (2007-12).

Despite legislation and laws for the empowerment of women, they are being exploited and sexually abused by the man-dominating society.

Discarded by the families and wondering further and further away from home, their real selves are lost or submerged under layers of dirt. They become non–persons, consciously ignored, paid unhealthy attention. Homelessness is a crucial issue for women. For women in difficult circumstances, SWADHAR HOME was launched by the Department of Women and Child Development in 2001-02. The scheme through the provisions of shelter, food, clothing, counselling, training, clinical and legal-aid aims to rehabilitate such women. The scheme is being implemented through States Government Agencies, Municipal Corporations and Voluntary Organisations. The present study is based on functioning of SWADHAR HOMES for the destitute women in Uttar Pradesh and Karnataka.

K.K. Srivastava

Acknowledgements

During the course of study, a considerable number of people have helped me owing to which I have been able to complete this work. I, therefore, gratefully acknowledge the contribution of each and every person. First of all, I am personally indebted to Prof. Emeritus Dr. S. N. Singh, Director, Institute for Applied Research and Development and reverend teacher for his dynamic advice, guidance and most valuable elderly concern for accomplishing this project. I, very personally and humbly feel obliged to Prof. K. Kishore, Head, Department of Public Administration, University of Lucknow, for valuable advice and discussion, finding time from her administrative and academic busy time schedule. I also acknowledge the contribution made by Prof. I.D. Mishra in terms of his valuable guidance and suggestions. I am thankful to Indian Council of Social Science Research (ICSSR), New Delhi for providing financial assistance for the study. I am thankful to the officials of states, districts and blocks, who directly and indirectly helped during the course of study. I am also thankful to Mr. M.C. Ramesh, General Secretary, Vidyaranya Education and Development Society (R) for his kind support.

My special thanks are to the members of the research team especially Dr. S.S. Chauhan, who took immense pain from his too busy schedule to complete the field work in time and later in compilation and tabulation of the data.

I would like to thank the library staff of the Department of Public Administration, University of Lucknow, particularly Mr. Y. P. Singh, Mr. Swarup Kishore and Mr. Mayank Srivastava for their sincere cooperation and encouragement in completing the work at the earliest.

Thanks are also due to Dr. A. K. Singh for conceiving the project and providing all types of support to complete the work. I am also thankful to Dr. Nimish Gupta for providing all types of technical support in processing data and compilation of book.

At last, but not least, I express my gratitude to all those who helped me particularly my colleagues and friends.

K.K. Srivastava

1

Introduction

Prelude

"We hereby adopt and commit ourselves as Governments to implement the following Platform for action, ensuring that a gender perspective is reflected in all our policies and programmes. We urge the United Nations' system, regional and international financial institutions, other relevant regional and international institutions and all women and men, as well as non-governmental organisations, with full respect for their autonomy, and all sectors of civil society, in cooperation with governments, to fully commit themselves and contribute to the implementation of this platform for Action."

Bejjing Declaration

The first United Nations World Conference on women was held in Mexico city in 1975, was followed by the United Nations, *Decade for Women; Equality, Development and Peace* (1976–85). The second conference held in Copenhagen in 1980, adopted a programme of action for the second half of the United Nations Decade for Women; Equality, Development and Peace, while the third conference, hosted by Kenya in 1985, adopted the

Nairobi Forward– looking strategies for the Advancement of Women to the year 2000.

The United Nations Development Fund for Women (UNIFEM), was born in response to the call of women from all over the world, a fund within the United Nations System, to aid and advocate for women of the developing world to give them voice and visibility. The fund was created to provide district support to women and to promote the inclusion of women in the decision-making process of mainstream development programmes.

The World Summit held during November, 25–28, 1996 at Trinidad and Tobago was the First Conference of Ministers Responsible for Women Affairs. Forty-five Commonwealth Countries participated and very useful decisions were taken regarding the implementation of Commonwealth Plan of Action on gender and development, gender management systems, gender integration into politics and women's human rights. The next meeting was held at Edinburgh in 1997. However, rigorous efforts are being made throughout the world and various schemes and programmes have been launched to minimise the gender-bias, and offer ample opportunities to bring women at par with men in respect of education, employment, human rights and decision-making roles etc.

Empowerment as a concept was first brought at the International Women's Conference in 1985 at Nairobi. The conference concluded that, empowerment is a redistribution of power and control of resources in favour of women through positive intervention.

The Programme of Action, 1992, has comprehensively given the below mentioned parameters of empowerment of women:

- Enhance self–esteem and self–confidence in women.

- Build a positive image of women by recognising their contribution to the society, polity and economy.
- Develop in them an ability to think critically.
- Faster decision-making action through collective process.
- Enable women to make informed in areas like education, employment and health especially reproductive health.
- Ensure equal participation in the development process.
- Provide information, knowledge and skill for economic independence.
- Enhance access to legal, literacy and information related to their rights and entitlements in the society with a view to enhance their participation on an equal footing in all areas.

The principle of gender equality is enshrined in the Indian Constitution in its Preamble, Fundamental Rights, Fundamental Duties and Directive Principles. The Constitution not only grants equality to women, but also empowers the State to adopt measures of positive discrimination in favour of women.

Within the framework of a democratic polity, our laws, development policies, plans and programmes have aimed at women's advancement in different spheres. From the Fifth Five Year Plan (1974 – 78) onwards there has been a marked shift in the approach to women's issues from welfare to development. In recent years, the empowerment of women has been recognised as the central issue in determining the status of women. The National Commission for Women was set up by an Act of Parliament in 1990 to safeguard the rights and legal entitlements of women. The 73rd and 74th Amendments

(1993) to the Constitution of India have provided for reservation of seats in the local bodies of Panchayats and Municipalities for women, laying a strong foundation for their participation in decision-making at the local levels.

India has also ratified various international conventions and human rights instruments committing to secure equal rights of women. Key among them is the ratification of the Convention on Elimination of All Forms of Discrimination Against Women (CEDAW) in 1993.

The Mexico Plan of Action (1975), the Nairobi Forward Looking Strategies (1985), the Beijing Declaration as well as the Platform for Action (1995) and the Outcome Document adopted by the UNGA Session on Gender Equality and Development and Peace for the 21st Century, titled "*Further actions and initiatives to implement the Beijing Declaration and the Platform for Action*" have been unreservedly endorsed by India for appropriate follow up. The women's movement and a wide-spread network of Non-Government Organisations which have strong grass-roots presence and deep insight into women's concerns have contributed in inspiring initiatives for the empowerment of women.

However, there still exists a wide gap between the goals of the Constitution, legislation, policies, plans, programmes and related mechanisms on the one hand and the situational reality of the status of women in India, on the other. This has been analysed extensively in the Report of the Committee on the Status of Women in India, "*Towards Equality*", 1974 and highlighted in the National Perspective Plan for Women, 1988–2000, the Shramshakti Report, 1988 and the Platform for Action, Five Years After – An Assessment".

Gender disparity manifests itself in various forms, the most obvious being the trend of continuously declining female ratio in the population in the last few decades.

Social stereo typing and violence at the domestic and societal levels are some of the other manifestations. Discrimination against girl children, adolescent girls and women persists in parts of the country.

The provision of educational opportunities for women has been an important part of the national endeavour in the field of education since India's independence. Though these endeavours did yield significant results, gender disparity persists with uncompromising tenacity, more so in the rural areas and among the disadvantaged communities. This is not only a matter of national anxiety and concern but also a matter of national conscience.

The underlying causes of gender inequality are related to social and economic structure, which is based on informal and formal norms, and practices. Consequently, the access of women particularly those belong to weaker sections including Scheduled Castes/Scheduled Tribes/ Other Backward Classes and minorities; majority of whom are in the rural areas and in the informal, unorganised sector need to be taken care of in education, health and productive resources, among others, is inadequate. Therefore, they remain largely marginalised, poor and socially excluded.

The goal of the National Policy on Women Empowerment (2001) is to bring about the advancement, development and empowerment of women. The policy widely disseminated so as to encourage active participation of all stakeholders for achieving its goals. Specifically, the objectives of this policy include:

i. Creating an environment through positive economic and social policies for full development of all women to enable them to realise their full potential.

ii. The *de-jure* and *de-facto* enjoyment of all human rights and fundamental freedom by women on equal basis with men in all spheres – political, economic, social, cultural and civil.

iii. Equal access to participation and decision-making of women in social, political and economic life of the nation.

iv. Equal access to women to health-care, quality education at all levels, career and vocational guidance, employment, equal remuneration, occupational health and safety, social security and public office etc.

v. Strengthening legal systems aimed at elimination of all forms of discrimination against women.

vi. Changing societal attitudes and community practices by active participation and involvement of both men and women.

vii. Mainstreaming a gender perspective in the development process.

viii. Elimination of discrimination and all forms of violence against women and the girl child; and

ix. Building and strengthening partnerships with civil society, particularly women's organisations.

Legal-judicial system has to be made more responsive and gender sensitive to women's needs, especially in cases of domestic violence and personal assault. New laws have to be enacted and existing laws reviewed to ensure that justice is quick and the punishment meted out to the culprits is commensurate with the severity of the offence.

Women's equality in power sharing and active participation in decision-making in political process at all levels should be ensured for the achievement of the goals of empowerment. All measures have to be taken to guarantee women's equal access to and full participation in decision-making bodies at every level, including legislative, executive, judicial, corporate, statutory bodies, as also the Advisory Commissions, Committees, Boards and Trusts etc. Affirmative action such as reservations/ quotas, including in higher legislative bodies, have to be considered whenever necessary on a time bound basis.

Women's perspectives have to be included in designing and implementing macro-economic and social policies by institutionalising their participation in such process. Their contribution to socio-economic development as producers and workers will be recognised in the formal and informal sectors (including home-based workers) and appropriate policies relating to employment and to her working conditions will be drawn. Such measures could include:

i. Reinterpretation and redefinition of conventional concepts of work wherever necessary e.g., in the Census records, to reflect women's contribution as producers and workers.

ii. Preparation of satellite and national accounts.

iii. Development of appropriate methodologies for undertaking (i) and, (ii) above.

Globalisation has presented new challenges for the realisation of the goal of women's equality, the gender impact of which has not been systematically evaluated fully. However, from the micro-level studies that were commissioned by the Department of Women and Child Development, it is evident that there is a need for re–framing policies for access to employment and quality of employment. Benefits of the growing global economy have been unevenly distributed leading to wider economic disparities, the feminisation of poverty, increased gender inequality through often deteriorating working conditions and unsafe working environment especially in the informal economy and rural areas. Strategies have to be designed to enhance the capacity of women and empower them to meet the negative social and economic impacts, which may flow from the globalisation process.

Equal access to education for women and girls is essential. Special measures have to be taken to eliminate discrimination, universalise education, eradicate illiteracy, create a gender-sensitive educational system, increase enrollment and retention rates of girls and improve the quality of education to facilitate life-long learning as well as development of occupation/vocation/technical skills by women. Reducing the gender gap in secondary and higher education has to be a focus area.

The holistic approach to women's health which includes both nutrition and health services has to be adopted and special attention has to be given to the needs of women and the girls at all stages of the life cycle. The reduction of infant mortality and maternal mortality, which are sensitive indicators of human development, has to be a priority of all concerns. Women should have access to comprehensive, affordable and quality health care.

Programmes have to be strengthened to bring about a greater involvement of women in science and technology. These will include measures to motivate girls to take up science and technology for higher education and also ensure that development projects with scientific and technical inputs involve women, fully. Efforts to develop a scientific temper and awareness will also be stepped up. Special measures have to be taken for their training in areas where they have special skills like communication and information technology.

All forms of violence against women, physical and mental, whether at domestic or societal levels, including those arising from customs, traditions or accepted practices should be dealt effectively with a view to eliminate its incidence. Institutions and mechanisms/

schemes for assistance have to be created and strengthened for prevention of such violence, including sexual harassment at work place and customs like dowry; for the rehabilitation of the victims of violence and for taking effective action against the perpetrators of such violence. A special emphasis has also to be laid on programmes and measures to deal with trafficking in women and girls.

Media should be used to portray images consistent with human dignity of girls and women. The policy of empowerment of women should specifically strive to remove demeaning, degrading and negative conventional stereotypical images of women and violence against women. Private sector partners and media networks will have to be involved at all levels to ensure equal access for women, particularly, in the area of information and communication technologies. The media should be encouraged to develop codes of conduct, professional guidelines and other self-regulatory mechanisms to remove gender stereotypes and promote balanced portrayals of women and men.

It is not the beliefs but the structures existing in the society that have caused the subordination of women. Beliefs are a reflection of the prevailing structures. A dalit believing that he is inferior and this is not the cause of his unequal status. The belief has been created by the existing caste and social structure and by the dominant people who gain from that structure. Patriarchy is the structure which has made women to believe that they are inferior to men. We are addressing this at different levels. The main impediment is our culture and tradition which further discriminates against women. Other factors such as the economic structure which favorus the men and the fact that, property, resources and assets belongs to men makes women vulnerable to violence, desertion and death. Increasing violence against women inside home, during riots or in conflict situations has also reduced women's freedoms and eroded their rights.

However, during the last decade, educational opportunities for women have dramatically increased and so have employment opportunities for women. The nutritional status of women within the household has improved. The women's movement spanning thirty years has given women rights. Men are now participating in the upbringing of children in better ways. But drought and forced migration with lack of negotiating skills have slowed the process of empowerment and even compelled people to enter dangerous occupations, including sex trade. Being in the unorganised sector has reduced the collective bargaining power of workers and further, privatisation has taken away social security benefits and reservations as well.

National Perspective

Throughout the Indian history, women have been treated as a deprived class. Hence, one of the major goals of Mahatma Gandhi throughout the nationalist movement was a sincere wish to achieve equality for women. In fact, his life mission was to bring women on equal footing with men which he declared in no uncertain terms.

"I am uncompromising in the matters of women's rights. In my opinion, she should labour under no legal disabilities, not suffered by men. I should treat the daughters and sons on a footing perfect equality."

Women were Gandhi's last persons whose tears he wanted to wipe-out and without whose liberation, he thought independence was superficial.

With the declaration of independence and transfer of political power, the pith and marrow of women's movement of yesterdays became suddenly subdued. Only a minority of erstwhile radical women leaders carried their activities beyond post-independence period. The Independence thus by no means improved the lives of women. Several barriers automatically, many old and many new stood in the way of improvement in the condition of women in different domains of their life.

Without doubt, Independence brought the promise of actual liberation and equality. And in the years following freedom, tremendous changes were felt in the status of women in Indian society. The first major document of the Constitution of India was adopted on January 26, 1950 which is the Article 15(3) that empowers the State to make any special provision for the welfare of women. Article 16(1) guarantees equality of opportunity for all citizens in matters relating to employment or appointment to any office under the State. And, Article 16(2) forbids discrimination in respect to any employment of office under the state on the grounds of sex. Then there are the Directive Principles some of which concern women indirectly or by necessary implication, while a few are women specific. The Directive Principles that concern women indirectly or by necessary implication include Article 38, which directs the state to secure a just social, political and economic order, geared to the welfare of the people. The Directive Principles which concern women directly and have a special bearing on their status include Article 39(a) right to an adequate means of livelihood for men and women equally, Article 39(d) equal pay for equal work for both men and women, Article 39(e) protection of the health and strength of worker men, women and children, and Article 42 providing for just humane conditions of work and maternity relief.

Policies and Programmes

Development of women has been receiving attention of the government right from the very **First Plan (1951-56)**.

In this plan, social welfare services were given in very comprehensive terms. The object of welfare is the attainment of social health which implies the realisation of such objectives as adequate living standards, the assurance of social justice etc. But the plan also envisages the welfare programmes of women. These programmes could not make much headway because of the inadequate administrative structure and meager financial allocations. The Control Social Welfare Board (CSWB), set-up in 1953, acts as an apex body at national level to promote voluntary action at various levels, especially welfare-related activities for women and children.

The **Second Five-Year Plan (1956-61),** emphasised that social welfare is concerned with the well-being of the entire community and not only of a particular sections of the population. It also focussed attention welfare programmes for women, physical and mental fitness, correctional administration and prohibition.

In the **Third Five-Year Plan (1961-66),** there was landmark development in the name of welfare. It was the establishment of Department of Social Welfare in the Central Government in 1964.

Fourth Five-Year Plan (1969-74), is mainly known for speeding up the Third Five-Year Plan which were planned earlier.

During **Fifth Five-Year Plan (1974–79),** removal of poverty and attainment of self-reliance was main objective. It emphasised the development and orientation approach and strategy for social welfare, besides giving priority to women's education, and launching measures to improve maternal and child health services, supplementary feeding for children and expectant and nursing mothers.

A new approach from welfare to development took place in **Sixth Five Year Plan (1980–85)**. According, the Sixth Plan adopted multi-disciplinary approach with special thought on the three core sectors of health, education and employment. In this plan eradication of poverty was main objective, by improving the quality of life. The schemes given priority were the Integrated Child Development Services, vocational training to women etc.

In the **Seventh Five-Year Plan (1985-90)**, the developmental programmes continued with the major objective of raising their economic and social status and bringing them into the mainstream of national development. A significant step in this direction was to promote the 'Beneficiary Oriented Schemes' (BOS) in various developmental sectors which extended direct benefits to women.

The **Eight Five Year Plan (1992-97)**, with human development as its major focus, played a very important role in the development of women. It promised to ensure that benefits of development from different sectors do not by-pass women, implement special programmes and to monitor the flow of benefits to women from other development sectors and enable women to function as equal partners and participants in the development process.

Two significant changes in the conceptual strategy of planning for women is the core feature of the **Ninth Five-Year Plan (1997-2002)**. Firstly, 'Empowerment of Women' became one of the nine primary objectives of the Ninth Plan. To this effect, the approach of the plan was to create an enabling environment where women could freely exercise their rights both within and outside home, as equal partners along with men. Secondly, the plan attempted 'convergence of existing service' available in both women-specific and women related sectors. To this effect, it directed both the centre and the states to adopt a special strategy of 'Women's Component Plan' (WCP) through which not less than thirty per cent of funds flow to women from all the general development sectors.

Major strategy of 'Empowering Women' as Agents of Social Change and Development was the main approach of Tenth Five-Year Plan (2002-2007). Empowering Women of National Policy is based on the following issues:

Social Empowerment: To create an enabling environment through various affirmative developmental policies and programmes for development of women besides providing them easy and equal access to all the basic minimum services so as to enable them to realise their full potentials.

Economic Empowerment: To ensure provision of training, employment and income generation activities with both 'forward' and 'backward' linkages with the ultimate objective of making all potential women economically independent and self-reliant.

Gender Justice: To eliminate all terms of gender discrimination and thus, allow women to enjoy not only the *de-jure* but *de-facto* rights and fundamental freedom on par with men in all spheres *viz,.* political, economic, social, civil, cultural etc.

The Eleventh Five-Year Plan (2007–12), emphasised more and more women empowerment plan and programme.

Ensuring economic empowerment, engineering social empowerment, enabling political empowerment, effective implementation of women-related legislations and creating institutional mechanisms for gender main-streaming and strengthening delivery mechanisms.

In this five year plan for the first time, women are recognised not just as equal citizens but as agents of economic and social growth. The approach to gender equally is based on the recognition that intervention in favour of women must be multi-pronged and they are: provide women with basic entitlements, address the reality of globalisation and its impact on women prioritising economic empowerment, ensure an environment-free from all forms of violence against women (VAW) physical, economic, social, psychological, ensure the participation and adequate representation of women at the highest policy levels, particularly in Parliament and State Assemblies, and, strengthen existing institutional mechanisms and create new ones for gender mainstream and effective policy implementation.

Noble laureate Rabindranath Tagore felt a pain and inequality of the situation more than half a century ago, thus:

"O Lord why have you not given
woman the right to conquer her destiny?
Why does she have to wait head bowed,
by the roadside,
waiting with tired patience,
hoping for a miracle in the morrow."

Country has made much more legislations for women. But mere legislations do not help women. It requires actions in the form of implementations and executions.

Legislations are made for the developments. But developments only reinforce the belief that laws alone do not lead to social transformation, unless followed by resolute action and social awareness of the wrong from time immemorial. An eminent jurist V. R. Krishna Iyer said, "The Constitutional provisions are weapons, not victories. Law has to be activated". In short, the struggle for justice, social, economic and political remains to be fought and won. In this scenario, all talk of women empowerment is nothing more than empty jargon. The situation demands a revolution of consciousness in the mind of women in the ways they think about themselves. According to Eleventh Plan Women are exempted from paying fees to fight eases of human rights violations. Plan tried to make more employment percentage of women in different sectors.

Indian National Council for women has made following suggestions to bridge the gap between theory and practice;

A. Empowerment should be viewed as a two-fold process. Constructive activities reorganise women's role system to be accompanied by effective interventions leading to the community internalising the idea of women's empowerment for its better future.

B. Providing economic and political strength to women through collective activities should be given the necessary focus. Clubbing of women's issues should be avoided.

C. The need for women to have social space like '*Sakhi Sabha*', '*Mahila Mandal*' etc. within the community set up through panchayat samities should be given due recognition. Formalisation of women NGOs network to play a catalytic role in the social transformation should be give due attention. Development of leadership among women for advancement of community is also necessary.

D. Communication within the women's organisation and the community at large has to be fostered.

The plight of women is distressing and their conditions in society are deplorable, notwithstanding the fact that there have been some improvements in the lives of negligible section of women. This improvement has been because of the measures taken for the amelioration of their lot by the governments, voluntary organisations and social groups. But there still remains a lot to be done to ensure a meaningful life for the womenfolk of our country.

Problems of Women

The problems of women may be enumerated briefly as follows:

(a) **Gender Bias:** Women in India suffer gender bias of extreme nature. They are discriminated on the basis of sex. Boys are preferred over girls as is evident from the female foeticide and infanticide, preference to boys interms of food, nourishment, education and other necessities of life.

(b) **Absence of Freedom:** Women do not enjoy as much freedom and liberty as men do. It is rightly observed that women have always to depend on their parents in their childhood and adolescence, on their husbands and in-laws after marriage and on their children in old age. Lack of freedom does not let their institutive qualities of assertion, leadership and enterprise to develop and blossom.

(c) **Crime against Women:** Through various types of crimes women are victimised. They are abused and exploited, physically and mentally tortured, beaten and even burnt for dowry, divorced in flimsy grounds and compelled to undergo all kinds of hardships if performing the dual tasks of breadwinners and carrying out domestic chores if employed. Abduction, rape, murder especially in disputes about property and of old single women by their domestic servants, and harassment at workplaces has become very common.

(d) **Poverty:** Women are the most impoverished, they live in object poverty, if alone they are not able to feed their children, sold by parents in exchange of money, forced to adopt prostitution and even being the object of human traffic to be exported to foreign countries.

(e) **Denial of Education:** Girls are denied education because they are destined to do household activities and are not supposed to be exposed, outside the four walls of the house.

(f) **Poor Facilities for Professional Training:** Even though girls in the towns go to schools they lack adequate facilities and avenues for training for higher education.

(g) **Absence of Employment Opportunities:** There is dearth of jobs for even educated women. Unemployment is the most serious problem, foreced to accept jobs at lower wages and on terms and conditions of the employer. They are denied economic and social security available to the regular employees in public services and organised sector of labour.

(h) **Social Evils:** Child marriage, expensive marriages involving expenditures beyond the capacity of some parents, large families, too many children despite the publicity for smaller families, joint family system expecting and forcing the women to be engaged in various household responsibilities, lack of leisure and recreational activities. Use of drugs and alcohol among the well to do family women, death of bread earners in riots and wars further augment the problems of women.

(i) **Absence of Proper Representation in Social, Economic and Political Institutions:** Women are denied proper representation and empowerment in social, economic and political institutions in the matters of decision-making and implementation of concerned policies and programmes. Though they have been given thirtythree per cent reservations at the grassroots institutions, their struggle for getting the same at State legislatures and Parliaments has not been successful so far.

Department of Women and Child Development (Ministry of Human Resource Development)

The Department of Women and Child Development is the nodal agency to implement and coordinate women related welfare and development programmes. It activates different Ministries and Departments both at the Centre and State levels respectively for the women's welfare and development programmes. The department plays vital role in implementing the following welfare programmes for women development:

A. Women Working Hostels

With the progressive change in the economic structure of the country, more and more women are coming out from their homes in search of employment. Main difficulties faced by them are lack of suitable accommodation in a healthy and wholesome environment. Keeping in view the challenges in terms of difficulties faced by such women, a Central Scheme of Assistance for construction of Hostel Buildings for working women was initiated in 1972. The development of women has always been the central focus in development planning since independence. Though there have been various shifts in policy approaches in the last 60 years from the concept of 'welfare' in 70s, to development in the 80s, and now to empowerment in 90s. The Department of Women and Child Development since its inception has been implementing special programmes designed to improve the socio-economic status of women. The scheme of Hostels for working women seeks to provide reasonable rented and safe accommodation to working women.

B. Employment and Training

The Programme of Support to Training–cum–Employment for Women (STEP) was launched in 1987 to strengthen and improve the skills for employment opportunities for women below poverty line, in traditional sectors of agriculture, small animal husbandry, dairying, fisheries, handlooms, handicrafts, cottage and village industries, sericulture, social foresting and waste land development where women are employed on a large scale. The focus is mainly on marginalised and assetless women, female headed households and women of other dispossessed groups.

The Scheme of Training–cum–Employment Production Centres the NORAD (Norweign Agency for International Development) assisted training programmes for women extends financial assistance to public-sector undertakings organisations to train women in traditional and non-traditional trades equip them for employment on a sustainable basis.

C. Socio-Economic Programme

Under the Socio-Economic Programme (SEP) initiated in 1958, voluntary organisations are given financial assistance to take up a wide variety of income generating activities which include the production of industrial components in ancillary units, handlooms, handicrafts, self-employment ventures like vegetable or fish vending etc.

D. Institutes for the Rehabilitation of Women in Distress

Recognising the need to prevent exploitation of women and to support their survival and rehabilitation, the scheme of Short Stay Home for women and girls was introduced as a social defence mechanism, by the Department of Social Welfare in 1969. Since 1999, the scheme of Short Stay Home (SSH) is being implemented by Central Social Welfare Board (CSWB) involving State Social Welfare Boards. Earlier, this scheme was implemented by the Department of Social Welfare and Women and Child Development. Under the scheme, temporary accommodation, maintenance and rehabilitative services are provided to women and girls rendered homeless due to family discord, crime, violence, mental stress, social ostracism or are being forced into prostitution and are in moral danger. Another scheme for Women in Difficult circumstances – SWADHAR with the similar objectives and target group was launched by the Department of Women and Child Development in 2001–2002. The scheme through the provisions of shelter, food, clothing, counselling, trainings, clinical and legal aid, aims to rehabilitate such women. The scheme is being implemented through State Government Agencies, Municipal Corporations and Voluntary Organisations.

In addition to the above, the Women Helplines are also being run by some organisations separately or with Swadhar Home.

E. *Indira Mahila Yojna*

The *Indira Mahila Yojna* (IMY) which aims at organising women at the grassroots level to facilitate their participation in decision-making, and their empowerment was launched on 2nd August, 1995, to start with, in 200 ICDS blocks. The objectives of the scheme are: convergence of the schemes of every sectoral department; awareness–generation among the women from rural areas and urban slums; and economic empowerment of women. It was recast as *Swayamsidha* in 2001 to empower women by generating awareness and helping them to achieve economic strength through micro-level income generation activities and facilitate easy convergence of various services such as literacy, health, non-formal education, rural development, water supply etc.

Swayamsidha is an integrated scheme for women's empowerment through formation of women into Self-Help Groups (SHGs). The scheme was launched in February 2001 across the States and Union Territories of the country.

Social Empowerment Schemes Swadhar

The *Swadhar* Scheme was launched by the Department during the year 2001-2002 as a Central Sector Scheme for providing holistic and integrated services to women in difficult circumstances, such as destitute widows deserted by these families in religious places like Vrindaban and Kashi, women prisoners released from jail and without family support; women survivors of natural disasters, who have been rendered homeless and are without any social and economic support trafficked women/girls, rescued or runaway from brothels or other places or victims of sexual crimes, who are disowned by family or who do not want to go back to their family for various reasons, women victims of terrorist violence who are without any family support, mentally challenged women who are without any support of family or relatives etc.

Short Stay Homes

The Scheme of Short Stay Homes was launched in the year 1969 with the objective to protect and rehabilitate those women and girls who are facing social, economic and emotional problems due to family stress, social ostracism, moral danger, etc. The programme was transferred to CSWB for implementation *w. e. f.* April 1999. Temporary shelter to the needy women and girls is given for six months to three years. Children accompanying the mother or born in the home may be permitted to stay in the home upto age of seven years, after which they may be transferred to children institutions or provided foster care services. The programme was transferred to CSWB in April 1999.

Family Counselling Centres

The objectives of Family Counselling Centres is to provide preventive and rehabilitative services to women and children who are victims of atrocities and family maladjustments. The Family Counselling Centre (FCC) scheme is being implemented through Central Social Welfare Board (CSWB) since 1984 through voluntary organisations. Family Counselling Centres are also being run for special categories of clients such as at police headquarters, FCCs in Mahila Jails, Rape Crisis Intervention Centres and Pre-Marital Counselling

Centres. Women's organisation and other voluntary social welfare organisations engaged in the work relating to women issues can avail grants from CSWB for setting-up Family Counselling Centres. The guarantee Institutions are also expected to make twenty per cent contribution to the budget sanctions.

Condensed Courses of Education of Women

The scheme of Condensed Courses of education implemented through the Central Social Welfare Board and aims to benefit needy women of tribal, hilly, backward areas and urban slums of the age fifteen years who would not join mainstream education system or drop outs by providing them opportunity for education at different levels–primary, middle/high school. The main objective of the scheme is to provide educational qualification and relevant skills to women in order to make them eligible for identifiable remuneration, work opportunities so as to facilitate their empowerment.

Awareness Generation Programme for Rural and Poor Women

The scheme of Awareness Generation Programme aims at generating awareness amongst women and community at large on rights, status and problems of women in particular and other social concerns. The programme enables women to organise themselves and strengthen their participation in socio-economic and political processes. Under the scheme, eight camps with two days follow up are conducted to provide a platform to women where they come together, exchange their experiences and ideas and in the process they develop an understanding of reality and are encouraged to tackle their problems themselves to fulfill their needs.

With the march of time and progress since independence, the woman has gradually come to acquire considerable emancipation from complexities and ills with which she had been suffering for long. Today's woman has become to have better acceptability and respectability, better status of equality with men, better rights and privileges, better opportunities and avenues in all walks of national sphere–social, economic and political.

In the emancipation and liberation of women, in the recognition of the legitimate place in the family and in the society, in the recognition and protection of her interests, rights and privileges and in the gradual enhancement of her status, the laws have played great role as an instrument of change. In this context, this particular study is based upon Empowerment of Destitute Women through *Swadhar* Shelter Homes which is run by Ministry of Women and Child Development, Government of India. The scheme envisages providing shelter, food, clothing and rehabilitation for their reintegration and empowerment. The proposed study purports to review the functioning of the Scheme and assessing the impact on the empowerment of destitute women.

Objectives

The main objectives of the study are as follows:

- To review policies, programmes and schemes of state Governments and Central Government for development and empowerment of women in difficult circumstances;
- To study the *modus operandi* of implementation of *Swadhar* Scheme in selected states;
- To examine the status of shelter, emotional support and counselling, arrangements of clinical, legal and other support to women for socio-economic rehabilitation of women in difficult circumstances;
- To assess the impact of scheme on rehabilitation of women in difficult circumstances;

- To examine the living conditions of women in difficult circumstances in the selected *Swadhar* Shelter Homes and also to assess the impact of the schemes on their living standards;
- To examine the problems in effective functioning of the *Swadhar* Scheme and also women inmates in their socio-economic rehabilitation;
- To suggest policy measures for effective and efficient functioning of *Swadhar* Scheme.

Research Methodology

Research is an academic activity. It comprises defining and re-defining problems, formulating hypothesis or suggested solutions, collecting, organising and evaluating data, making deductions and reaching on conclusions, and at last carefully testing the conclusions to determine whether they fit the formulated hypothesis. It is an original constitution to the existing stock of knowledge making for its advancement. The purpose of research is to discover answers to question through the application of scientific procedure. The main aim of research is to find out the truth which is hidden and which has not been discovered as yet.

The study is based upon quantitative approach. It involves the generation of data in quantitative form which is subjected to rigorous quantitative analysis in a formal and rigid manner. It is further sub-classified into inferential, experimental and simulation approaches to research. The inferential approach to research is to form a database from which to infer characteristics or relationships of population. This usually means survey research where a sample of population is studied to determine its characteristics, and it is then inferred that the population has the same characteristics. Thus, research is the fountain of knowledge for the sake of knowledge and an important source of providing guidelines for solving different business, governmental and social problems.

The study is empirical in nature and is based on mainly primary data collected through field survey. The study is conducted in the states of Uttar Pradesh and Karnataka. The study covered a sample of 14 *Swadhar* Shelter Homes, 12 Helplines, 438 Women Inmates and 42 Officials and Non–officials. The survey is conducted with the help of structured interview schedule for shelter homes, operators of helpline, women inmates and officials and non–officials. Besides, collection and analysis of primary data, secondary data and pertinent literature is compiled from published and documented sources for insight stimulation. The policy measures are based on analysis of research findings and critical appreciation of pertinent literature.

As mentioned above that the study is conducted in two different states of Uttar Pradesh and Karnataka. The purpose of selection of Uttar Pradesh is that scholar belongs to this particular state which is known as BIMARU and most backward state. Because of development process is very slow in comparison to southern states. Development in terms of IT sector, civic sense, work culture, accountability, transparency and overall good governance. Though in the politics Uttar Pradesh plays a vital role in strengthening centre. So far Karnataka is concerned, it is known as developed states in all wakes of development and good governance, such as literacy rate, work to rule, IT sector etc. And above all geographical distribution is also one of the main parameters.

As far as in social science research, it is impossible to cover the whole universe. When field studies are undertaken in practical life, consideration of time and cost almost invariably lead to a selection of respondents *i.e.,* selection of only a few items.

2

Women and Common Economic Issues

An analysis of the detailed description of the trade groups taken up for study, reveals certain common economic issues which pre-dominate the lives of poor, self-employed women.

Low income is one of the basic issues for these women. They can barely eke out a living and are constantly worried about being able to make both ends meet. Even basic needs of food, clothing and shelter are not met from the money got from most of the trades. The nature of their work is such that there is an *inherent uncertainty* about the income they will earn in a particular time period. Being self-employed, they have learnt to live with this uncertainty. The number of days they will be able to find work, even in activities where they provide only labour, is not known to these women. Where they will get work, how much they will get paid, what will be the going rate, are all not known (as in agricultural labour, construction work, brick-making, etc). Whether they will be physically fit and therefore able to work when they find some, whether their family will be able to survive till some work is available, are serious doubts which are constantly preying on their minds. For those who invest their own funds and resources, the uncertainty is concerned with the prices they will be able to get for their products; what and how many raw materials they will be able to collect or get; how much they will be able to buy; how much they will be able to process; whether they will be able to sell their produce; and whether they will be able to recover their costs and earn something. The question of good health is of as much concern for own account workers as it is for those who provide labour (as in bamboo work, reed work, leather work, vegetable growing etc).

The *work opportunities* are restricted to their caste-based occupation or to physical, labour-intensive, unskilled work. Those who have been able to learn the caste-based occupation have an additional skill, other than physical labour. But many do not even know their caste-based occupation (such as, weaving). Women particularly, have little scope of getting work opportunities, than unskilled male labour. Even in caste-based occupations or family-based production units, the women do the unskilled and tiring labour work. The traditional division of labour is such that they do not get a chance to learn the whole work process (as in pottery, weaving and leather work). They, can, therefore earn a livelihood only from whatever skills they have. To the extent that a particular skill is viable in terms of demand and supply, in terms of its earning capacity, it enables them to survive. If the skill becomes obsolete, they are pushed to the brink of starvation (as in weaving, and cotton-boll shelling). This scarcity of work opportunity is one of the main causes for the low income they draw.

Landlessness and *lack of assets* are problems for the poor. Very few families of the lower castes (who make up the majority of the poor) have land. The few that do own land have such meager holding that their families are unable to draw sustenance from the land alone. The land is rarely in the name of the women. Their ownership of assets is also very limited. Whatever capital, cattle, or property (housing), or equipment for production, is owned by the family, is in the name of the men.. The asset base is also very minimal. It is more often than not handed down from their ancestors. If they had to purchase such assets today, it would be almost impossible for them to do so, on their own. Only if they are able to get the benefit of some development programme would they be able to procure new assets (loans for equipment, cattle, housing facilities, land from the Land Ceiling Act)?

The *status of women* in the village depends on whether they are daughters or daughters-in-law of that particular village. Traditionally, the daughter is not married off in the same village. The adult female population in a village is mostly of women, who have come to the village after getting married—the daughters-in-law. It is very rare to find adult daughters in the female population of the village because girls are normally married off in their teens. Only in cases where daughters have been deserted by their husbands, or are widowed, have they come to stay at their parental home. Unmarried adult daughters are very rare. The activities in which adult women are involved are thus pursued mainly by the daughters-in-law. They are not allowed as much freedom as the daughters. They also have the additional roles of wife, mother, and home-maker to fulfill along with their role of worker. They are expected to contribute to the family income among the poor. If they do not have any income generating skills, these are taught them. Educating (to pursue a trade) the daughter-in-law is seen as a permanent asset for the family. The daughters constitute the adolescent female population of the village.

Their *work skills* are *acquired* mainly from the family (parental or marital), neighbour, or friends. As such, they do not know where else to acquire new skills if the skills they have are not viable any more. They do not have easy access to training programmes, nor do they know of the existence of many such facilities. The women, particularly, are quite unaware of the avenue that may be open for acquiring new skills, even when they are willing to learn. Sewing machines and *charkha* spinning have come to symbolise the need of the women to acquire new skills, because they are the avenues which the women have seen and made use of in their own experience. Even if the women know of the new skills which can help them, they do not know the procedure followed at various levels, to get training facilities. They have perforce to operate through their husbands.

Those engaged in providing labour have to maintain contact with gang leaders or retain friendly relations with farmers and others who need work to be done. As there is no employer-employee relationship with any one person, they have to ensure that their work opportunities continue indefinitely. If they do not have stable contacts with those who need labour services, the women (along with the mean) have to go from site to site, on farm to farm, asking if their services are needed (as in migrant labour, construction work and brickmaking).

Similarly, those who are own account workers, have to maintain their contact with the sources of raw materials, funds, and equipment. They also have to maintain cordial relations with the purchasers of their products so that their market is ensured (as in bamboo work, pottery, reed work, leather work, weaving, vegetable growing, poultry and milk production).

Usually, however, these contacts are managed by the men, especially, when it involves people outside the village. Within the village, the men relate to the men and the women to the women. With gang-leaders, the women usually operate through their men. If these relationships are not maintained, the own account workers have to deal with even greater uncertainties as far as their income is concerned or, they have to find new sources for the inputs, or forego their trade altogether and find other work (as in reed work, leather work, vegetable growing, agricultural labour and construction work).

They *prefer the customers to come to them* to procure what they need (agricultural labour, construction work, pottery, leather work, milk products, bamboo work). This is a way of ensuring that they have the final say in the rates or prices quoted. If the customer comes to them, the customer is acknowledging his/her need for the good or services. If such a situation does not arise, and they are desperate, they do go to the customers to sell their goods and services. This situation is perceived as a distress sale situation and is only resorted to in extremely dire situation. But when they have no choice, they are forced to take-up this option. The customer has the final say in quoting the rates and prices in such cases (migrant laour, brick-making, construction work, vegetable selling, reed work, bamboo work, pottery). The workers do not have much bargaining power when the staying power (to hold on to goods and services) in exhausted. They have to recover their investment and/or earn income to survive and thus, to compromise on the prices of their goods and the rates of their labour.

A low income for the women means a *low income for the whole family* because, very rarely, does the *income* come in the *hands of the women*. They are workers, beyond doubt, but they do not always control the income directly. In own account work they mainly work as one member of a family unit. In labour work, they have a greater opportunity to work in an individual capacity. Nevertheless, the income is seen as family income, even if it is income for the basic needs of the family. When the money available to them is not enough to meet their basic needs, the family has to borrow funds.

Credit is not easily available to the poor in rural areas. Credit from private sources (money-lenders and others) is very strictly controlled. Only those who have material assets, such as, land and cattle are considered creditworthy. The poor women, and especially those belonging to the lower castes, are not trusted in money matters. Most of them do not own land or other assets and it is, therefore very difficult for them to get credit. They can borrow small amounts (Rs 20 or Rs 25) as advance payment on work on a personal basis. It has, however, to be repaid within a few days. Larger amounts are quite out of the question. If their relationship with the well-off is particularly good, they can borrow a couple of hundred rupees on personal surety. For most of the poor families, even amounts of a few hundred rupees are available only by pledging ornaments, utensils, or other such belongings. Loans are normally for a short duration, between three and six months only and the interest rates vary between Rs 2 and Rs 10 per month, for every hundred that is loaned. If the interest and principal are not repaid within the stipulated period, the articles pledged are sold. Because of these stringent terms the poor are very wary of borrowing on interest. As it is, they are reluctant to pledge it. The uncertainty of their income does not encourage them to pledge whatever little they may own. Only if they are very certain of being able to pay it back, do they borrow on interest. That, or they have to be very desperate indeed. They will then be reconciled to the possibility of selling off their ornaments. Pledging them is only a way of buying more time—if they are able to earn and repay to loan, the ornaments can be recovered. The condition of advancing money only for short duration is adhered to because of the inherent uncertainty of work and income in self-employment. Both lender and borrower are aware of it. In some cases, the loan is made for a period of a year but never more than that. The loans are also taken in kind—usually grains for consumption. These have to be repaid in kind—usually one and a half, or twice the quantity borrowed. The repayment is normally during harvest time. In other cases, the loan is in cash but the repayment and interest, in kind. All these negotiations are normally finalised between the men. The involvement of women is not encouraged.

Loans from banks are also available to rural people only in principle, however. The reason for initiating rural credit facilities through credit societies and nationalised banks, made available through development programmes, has been made in order to facilitate the flow of funds to the villagers. This laudable goal, however, does not actually reach the poor, particularly the women. The procedural requirements, the certifying and attestations necessary (from the *sarpanch* and *talati*), the need for surety, all of these make bank loans almost inaccessible to the poor. Even if they get the bank loans, the women are not given credit facilities. It is the privilege of men alone. The strained relationship between the lower and upper castes; the unwillingness of those with influence to let development agencies with the power elite of the villages; the ignorance of the poor people regarding schemes and procedures; all these ensure that the avenue of bank loans is effectively, close to the poor. Unless there is active intervention from women's organisations to divert bank facilities to women under the development programmes, the poor, rural women do not have access to them.

The transactions of poor, self-employed people (rural and urban, men and women) are usually *verbal*. This is because they deal with very few people, with people known within their reference system. The amounts involved are also small. The rural women are quite well-versed with conducting verbal transactions as well as the safeguards to be respected in such dealings. Being illiterate is not a handicap in such transactions because reading and writing are not necessary. Nor is it necessary to know procedural details, to have contact with officials, or information about various programmes and schemes. But the development programmes, the schemes for assistance, the rules, the procedures, the sanctioning of assistance, the evidence required to establish genuineness, all require the poor, self-employed to be proficient in written transactions. Written authentication, written applications, written forms, written sanctions, written records and testimonials, are the basis for such assistance. The women are handicapped by this shift from verbal to written. As far as their own work-related transactions are concerned, they can still survive by verbal dealings. But their work opportunities, their prospects for improving their situations, have become inextricably linked with official development efforts (governmental and non-governmental). For this, they have to acquire proficiency in written transactions. The women (and even the men) have neither any direct information about the schemes and facilities available, nor do they know in detail the procedural formalities to be followed. They do not even have any clout with the power elite in the village or the various offices which would help them overcome their handicap. Not being literate, then, becomes a serious constraint. They can be cheated and can be fooled.

This *general lack of awareness* of detailed procedures and formalities extends to other fields as well. Those engaged in providing labour do not always know the minimum rates which are applicable to them, they do not know of their rights regarding shelter, sanitation, child-care, leave, health, and accident compensation. Those who need their services are able to manipulate them and play upon their ignorance (as in migrant labour, construction work, digging mud, and agricultural labour).

Women work mainly as *member of the family unit* in own account work. They do not know all the stages of the work because the work of men and women is divided in such a way that women get to specialise only in activities requiring manual labour. The activities requiring dealings with the outside world, such as, procuring raw materials from the market, going to sell the products in the markets in town, are all handled by the men (as in weaving, bamboo work, vegetable growing and grocery stall keeping). The women are not able to get a sense of the market forces; they do not get an opportunity to acquire these skills. Even within the production process, quite often women cannot handle all the details independently (as in pottery, leather and bamboo work). The work of the women is viable only as a family unit and not independently as of individuals. Their sense of confidence, of being able to work individually, is, therefore, not very developed.

Raw material can be got from the collection, in exchange for a service, or, alternatively for cash (reed work, leather work, processing milk and bamboo work). Women are familiar with the social mechanism of free collection and also of getting raw materials in exchange for a service. They can produce these raw materials even without the men. When the raw materials are owned by the family, of course, then the women are comfortable.

But when it comes to buying raw materials (with cash) from the market then women feel handicapped. Similarly, for the selling of finished goods, women only feel comfortable when they sell it retail in their own or neighbouring villages (as vegetable growing). They do not, however, go to town to sell wholesale. Their links with the larger markets are very minimal. Their illiteracy, and inability to counting, is a great deterrent. Those who can count do go out of their own village. This is really a matter of getting exposed to the outside world. The men are also largely illiterate but have learnt, through experience, how to handle dealings (in a limited manner) in the larger markets.

The shortage of raw materials and the escalating prices are yet another issue for the women. They feel increasingly the impact of the raw materials they need being used for the industrial manufacturer of goods – bamboo, yarn, leather, straw, paddy husk. The supply/demand position of the new materials affects the prices. There are no facilities available for transportation of raw materials and finished goods. It can become uneconomical to pursue certain trades with only a small capital if the cost of raw materials and transportation goes too high. The poor are not always able to buy raw materials cheaply and get a reasonable price for the finished goods (bamboo work, weaving). Since their returns depend on the economical use of raw materials, the purchase price and sale price, they do not think several of the activities even worth an effort. Others, in the same activity, are able to earn least enough to subsist because they have been able to make a niche for themselves. All these efforts of locating cheap sources and good markets have to be made by the family on their own, without any assistance from anywhere. If they are able to establish contact, they are able to earn. Otherwise they are left to their fate. The women's role in making these contacts is not very great. Women are also not very familiar with accounting and costing methods.

Being exposed to only a very limited sphere of a large economy and having only one or two basic skills, they are not able to monitor market changes, product demand changes, and the nature of competition which comes in from factory-made goods or substitute products. Consequently, they are not able to make adjustments to their niche in the market or even to consistently protect their earnings and income. They are not able to monitor the influence policy changes which have an impact on them (bamboo forecast being leased to paper mills, podless cotton seeds being promoted, fodder for animals going to strawboard units).

The skills they have and the services they provide are viable only in a subsistence economy where the free collection and barter of goods and services is common. Products and by–products which were needed as inputs only in traditional skills are now in demand for other purposes as well (bamboo, leather, straw). There is a cash value available for bye-products which did not have any such demand earlier (reeds, straw). This changed profile of raw material consumption creates forces of commercialisation. Even the original users of raw materials, who used to get them free, now have to pay a cash price for them (clay, reeds). The selling price of their goods does not rise much and therefore, their trade becomes unviable because it cannot absorb the cash cost of raw materials. This interplay of commercial forces in a traditional, subsistence economy, affects the very survival of the poor. The women are worst affected because they do not even have access to the training and acquiring of new skills. There is continuous displacement of women from trades which are being rendered unviable due to commercialisation, mechanisation and competitive products coming into the market (weaving, pottery, tanning leather, reed work, bamboo work, making milk products). When new products processes are introduced in a particular trade, the men get the opportunity to learn the new methods but the women get pushed out of work completely (leather tanning, weaving). Women are reduced to working an unskilled labour wherever work is available, if it is available.

Whenever work is available, the cash does not usually go to the women. When men and women work together as labourers, the payment is more often than not made to the men. When women work as part of a family products unit, the cash goes to the person who goes to sell the products – which, more often than not is the man (weaving, bamboo work, pottery). When women work alone, the cash does come to them (reed work, grocery stalls). Various forms of *jajmani* system are still prevalent in the rural areas. Payment is often made either in kind or combination of cash and kind (pottery, agricultural labour, reed work). Payment made in grain certainly helps in consumption, but the present day economy demands cash transactions for purchases. Travelling to town, buying clothes, buying inputs for their trade, expenses for children's education, materials for housing, taxes, loan installments etc. all have to be paid in cash. They need a source of cash income much as they might value payment in kind. They have to find sources of work which will earn them some cash (usually labour work).

If work opportunities are not available in their own village, they are forced to migrate, in search of work. Sometimes, the men alone migrate and women stay back in the village (agricultural labour). In other cases the whole family migrates to wherever work is available (brick making, construction work, agricultural labour). The women have to bear the burden of migration. They have to learn to make house in the open, in strange places, in the fields, on construction sites, on brick-kiln sites. They learn to live with the bare minimum as well as accept an almost nomadic life style. Even facilities like water, sanitation, fuel and rations are managed with great difficulty and it is women who have to bear most of this burden.

Women have to work for very long hours combining both income-generating and household work. They usually have a work day of fourteen or fifteen hours and in places where the infrastructural facilities are very few, their work day stretches up to seventeen or eighteen hours. Looking after children and the family is a constant worry for them. If they can avoid going out of house to work, they prefer it but with the work opportunities being so few they have little choice to go out looking for work. Of the fifteen trades taken up for study, ten are home-based activities (except agricultural labour, construction work, digging mud, brick making and vegetable growing). This shows the significance of home-based work for poor, rural women. It is one way in which they can combine their various roles (social and work) with relative ease. It is only when they are unable to earn a livelihood from a home–based activity that they go out for work. Even when they migrate in search of work, they are constantly on the look for opportunities which will enable them to pursue home based activity. If they are able to work out some way by which to earn a livelihood by working at home, they stop migrating altogether.

The common pattern today is to pursue two or three seasonal income-generating activities to maximise earnings. The caste-based occupations are not pursued singly but interspersed with agricultural or other labour work. Some livestock is also tended side by side, such as, poultry, goats or cattle. Seasonal work opportunities are fully availed of wherever they are available. The uncertainty of returns from a particular trade is dealt with to some extent by pursuing more than one activity. They spread out their risks and try to ensure some inflow of cash as well as an income in kind, for the family. This is a survival strategy to manage every kind of contingency.

All the self-employed women have to make their own provisions for meeting the exigencies and contingencies of life. They are not entitled to any assistance if they are own account workers. If they are labourers, they are entitled, in some cases, to certain facilities but rarely get them. Health is a major concern for them because their body is their main asset and they have to pay for their medicines etc. They are also to earn a livelihood if their health does not desert them. The cost of dealing with occupational hazards is also borne by the workers themselves. Similarly, expenses for children's vocational education, housing, social occasions, are all met from their own resources.

Women in most trades do not have representative organisation to help them protect their interests. Rarely some women enrolled as members, even when representative organisations do exist, such as, those for brick workers, and milk producers. Traditionally, many of the trades studied here, have had guides to protect the interests of workers (bamboo workers, weavers, leather workers, potters). These guides have disintegrated today. Their link with the policy-making process is almost absent and consequently, they are unable to influence the policies that are formulated. They are not able to counter policies made against them either.

The raw materials and finished products have an intricate rural–urban network. Several raw materials are found only in the rural areas and the products are also consumed in only the villages (reed work, pottery). Other products are consumed primarily in the urban areas (brick work). Yet others are consumed in both the urban and rural areas (weaving, leather work). There are also products which use raw materials from other regions. The raw materials are sold in the urban areas and processed in the rural areas (bamboo work–sirkis). The finished products are consumed both in the urban and rural areas.

There is also a chain to urban to rural connections for some raw materials. Cotton for instance, is grown in villages. The cotton-bolls are shelled in the villages and then in ginning are done in urban areas. The spinning is done in the textile mills and on *charkhas* (in towns and villages). The yarn is used for mill production in the towns and for khadi and handloom in the villages. The cloth produced is used in the villages and towns.

This kind of network exists for other raw materials and finished goods too. Agricultural labour, for instance is concentrated in the villages. But the produce of agriculture is consumed in both rural and urban areas. The inputs for agriculture – seeds, fertilizers, pesticides – are produced both in the urban and rural areas. Similarly, construction work sites are located in both urban and rural areas, even though the labour force is mainly from the rural areas. The facilities created – roads, dams – benefit both the rural and urban population, but not necessarily the poor families in either region. Brick making needs the labour and some of the raw materials of rural areas. Other inputs like broken coal and cinder are bye-products of production units in urban areas. The bricks are consumed mainly in the urban areas and large construction activities like dams in the rural areas. Leather is a raw material of rural areas but the finished goods are used in the urban areas. The bamboo products, cloth, reed work, pottery, milk products, and vegetables are used in both urban and rural areas. The raw materials are brought sometimes from other regions. Grocery stalls bring goods produced in the urban to rural areas and also redistribute rural products.

There is a greater variety of influences acting on the prices, at different stages in the chain, in such cases. The availability, prices, and supply–demand position fluctuate quite a lot and the rural women do not understand this network very well.

Similarly, they view other villages and the urban areas as a large mass of inhabitation. They try and keep abreast of what kinds of goods and services are available in various villages and towns (black smiths, carpenters, potters, weavers, tools, chemicals, bamboo, yarn etc.). If they need a particular kind of facility, they usually make attempts to find out which village or town it is available in. The men are more informed than the women in these matters. But through their men, the women do come to know something. Knowing what is available where, is helpful in making decisions about whether they can afford it, whether they can find other ways of obtaining it etc. It provides a basis for reality orientation and an estimate of how much effort will be involved in obtaining the facility.

The women labour keep on working as long as they are capable, irrespective of their age. As long as they have strength in their bodies, they can pursue their trade and work. In poor family, the aged feel that they should also contribute to the household income. They are not able to be as active as the young but they do not wish to be a burden on the family, either. They also need to eat and poverty often blunts the human relationships of the aged, even with their own family. They find their own ways of maintaining dignity and not being a burden. Less exhaustive activities like poultry, reed work, cotton-boll shelling and milk production are pursued by the old. Their children may or may not live with them, but they still try to earn their keep. Often they look after the infants in family which enables the adults to go out for work. They may even accompany their children to the work sites and look after the children there. This kind of mutual help makes it easier for the old women to stay with their family.

The traditional system encourages self-employment for most people in the villages and urban areas. This point is also obvious from the negligible number of people who have regular salaried jobs with an established employer–employee relationship, in the villages. The forces of mechanisation and industrialisation, termed modernisation, are slowly changing the system. More and more work opportunities are being created. In fact, the training programmes, the schemes, the development activities view the whole workforce to be in need of jobs. Hence, plans are formulated with the objective of providing jobs for people. The plan is to ensure that everyone has a job. The fact is however, the most of the women (and men) are not seeking jobs – they are seeking work and income. The schemes and programmes which are started in the name of modernisation do not realise that they were shifting the trend from self-employment to other employment. The people's aspirations are centred on self-employment and the schemes, therefore, constantly face the problems of low productivity, low integrity and a lack of work identity when they provide jobs. The same trade followed on the principle of self-employment has different dynamics on the same place (weaving, bamboo work).

Another drawback with the development programmes is that they are worked out with the reality of the well-off people in mind. First instance, the bankable scheme for poultry is worked out on the basis of a poultry farm having several hundred birds. This is the way a well-off person would raise poultry. But the way the poor pursue the same activity is quite different. The poor economise on every front in order to maximise their return from a given investment. They can make poultry profitable even with an investment less than Rs 100. The poultry farm schemes worked out by the development agencies would be profitable only with the investment of several thousand rupees. Such schemes are totally beyond the capacity of the poor and it is not wonder that they are not accepted by the poor. The conclusions drawn by the development experts are that the scheme is unsuccessful and it is, therefore, dropped. The fact, very often, is that the scheme itself is not suitable to the needs of the poor. There is a big gap in the designing of the scheme and the way in which the poor engage in the work concerned. The economics would be minimal and within reach of the poor, the schemes should be designed keeping in mind the way a poor family functions.

3

Swadhar Shelter Home

Swadhar Shelter Home is a Central Sector Scheme. The scheme envisages merger of two ongoing Central Sector Schemes namely Swadhar and Short Stay Home that are being implemented across the country. Short Stay Home has been in operation since 1969 and *Swadhar* Scheme since 2001–2002. The merged new schemes have hundred per cent funding from the centre. *Swadhar* and Short Stay Home merger scheme converted into new nomenclature *Swadhar* Shelter Home.

Recognising the need to prevent exploitation of women and to support their survival and rehabilitation, the scheme of Short Stay Home for women and girls was introduced as a social defence mechanism by the Department of Social Welfare in 1969. Since 1999, the scheme of Short Stay Home is being implemented by Central Welfare Board (CSWB) involving State Social Welfare Boards. Earlier, this scheme was implemented by the Department of Social Welfare and Women and Child Development. Under the schemes, temporary accommodation, maintenance and rehabilitative services are provided to women and girls rendered homeless due to family forced into prostitution and are in mortal danger. Another scheme for women in Difficult Circumstances

Swadhar with similar objectives and target group was launched by the Department of Women and Child Development in 2001–2002. The scheme is being implemented through State Government Agencies, Municipal Corporation and Voluntary Organisations. In addition to the above, the Women Helplines are also being run by some organisations separately or with *Swadhar* home.

The Parliamentary Standing Committee on Ministry of Women and Child Development also recommended merger of Short Stay Home (SSH) and S*wadhar* in its 189th and 219th Reports. Merger of the two schemes has also been recommended in the mid-term appraisal of the XIth Plan. There is no financial onus on States in implementation of these schemes.

Swadhar as well as Short Stay Home schemes have been included in the XIth Five Year Plan. An amount of Rs 108 crore and Rs 154 crore had been earmarked for the XIth Five Year Plan period under *Swadhar* and *Swadhar* Shelter Home respectively. During the financial year 2010–11, the budget estimates for *Swadhar* and *Swadhar* Shelter Home is Rs 34.2 crore and Rs 25.75 crore respectively.

Under Swadhar Greh Scheme, budgetary allocation is Rs 21.32 lakh for 50 women.

The scheme is intended to provide immediate shelter, food, counselling, medical treatment etc. to women who are in difficult circumstances such as widows, destitutes and deserted women etc including those trafficked and rescued from brothels.

Each project seeks to improve the life of women, who are in difficult circumstances thereby making them self-reliant by providing vocational training. The women and girls rendered homeless due to family discord, crime, violence and mental stress will be able to reintegrate with their families through counselling. This helps immensely in socio–economic development of such women in particular and the country in general.

Swadhar Greh– A Scheme for Women in Difficult Circumstances

A. Background

Recognising the need to prevent women from exploitation and to support their survival and rehabilitation, the scheme of *Short Stay Home* for women and girls was introduced as a social defence mechanism, by the Department of Social Welfare in 1969. The scheme is meant to provide temporary accommodation, maintenance and rehabilitative services to women and girls rendered homeless due to family discord, crime, violence, mental stress, social ostracism or are being forced into prostitution and are in mortal danger. Another scheme with the similar objectives namely *Swadhar – A Scheme for Women in Difficult Circumstances* was launched by the Department of Women and Child Development in 2001-02. The scheme through the provisions of shelter, food, clothing, counselling, trainings, clinical and legal aid aims to rehabilitate such women in difficult circumstance.

Centre for Market Research and Social Development, New Delhi, conducted an evaluation in 2007 to assess the performance of both the schemes. The evaluation report while citing the effectiveness and positive impact of measures adopted under the schemes for counselling and rehabilitation found that the profile and category of residents, admission procedure, counselling, quality of service, vocational training, rehabilitation and follow up procedure are almost similar in both the schemes. It, therefore, recommended merger of these two schemes for better functioning and outcomes with lesser administrative burdens and procedures. It also recommended that the new scheme should focus on establishing one such home in every district.

The positive findings of the evaluation study has encouraged the Ministry to propose this new scheme that would target the women victims of unfortunate circumstances who are in need of institutional support for rehabilitation so that they could lead their life with dignity.

B. Vision

The scheme envisions a supportive institutional framework for woman victim of difficult circumstances so that she could lead her life with dignity and conviction. It envisages that shelter, food, clothing, and health as well as economic and social security are assured for such women. It also envisions that the special needs of these women are properly taken care of and under no circumstances they should be left unattended or abandoned which could lead to their exploitation and desolation.

C. Objectives

Under the scheme, new swadhar greh will be set up in every district with capacity of 30 women with the following objectives:

- To cater to the primary need of shelter, food, clothing, medical treatment and care of the women in distress and who are without any social and economic support.
- To enable them to regain their emotional strength that gets hampered due to their encounter with unfortunate circumstances.
- To provide them with legal aid and guidance to enable them to take steps for their readjustment in family/ society.
- To rehabilitate them economically and emotionally.
- To act as a support system that understands and meets various requirements of women in distress.
- To enable them to start their life afresh with dignity and conviction.

For big cities and other districts having more than 40 lakh population or those districts where there is a need for additional support to the women, more than one swadhar greh could be established. The capacity of swadhar greh could be expanded up to 50 or 100 on the basis of need assessment and other important parameters.

D. Strategies

The objectives cited above would be pursued adopting the following strategies:

- Temporary residential accommodation with or without the provision of food, clothing, medical facilities etc.
- Vocational and skill up gradation trainings for economic rehabilitation of such women.
- Counselling, awareness generation and behavioral training.
- Legal aid and Guidance.
- Counselling will also be provided through telephone.

E. Beneficiaries

The benefit of the scheme could be availed by women above 18 years of age of the following categories:

- Women who are deserted and are without any family support;
- Widows survivors of natural disaster who have been rendered homeless and are without any social and economic support;
- Women affected by HIV/AIDS;
- Women prisoners released from jail and are without family, social and economic support;
- Women victims of domestic violence, family tension or discord, are made to leave their homes without any

means of subsistence and have no special protection from exploitation and/or facing litigation on account of marital disputes; and

- Trafficked women/girls rescued or run-away from brothels or other places where they face exploitation. However such women/ girls should first seek assistance under Ujjawala Scheme in areas where it is in operation.

Women affected by domestic violence could stay up to one year. For other categories of women, the period of stay could be up to three years. The older women above the 55 years of age may be accommodated for maximum period of five years after which they will have to shift to old age home or such other institution.

Swadhar greh facilities could also be availed by the children accompanying women in the above categories. Girls up to the age of 18 years and boys up to the age of 12 years would be allowed to stay in the swadhar greh with their mothers. (Boys of more than 12 years of age will be shifted to the Children Homes being run under JJ Act).

F. Implementing Agencies and Eligibility Criteria

Any of the following agencies/organisations can seek assistance under the scheme:

- State Government agencies including Women Development Corporations set up by the State Government.
- Urban Municipal Bodies.
- Cantonment Boards.
- Panchayati Raj Institutions and Co-operative institutions.
- Departments of Women and Child Development/ Social Welfare in the State Governments which may

construct swadhar greh, and lease them to organisation(s) having requisite experience for such period as deemed fit, for managing the operations under this scheme.

- Public Trusts registered under any law for the time being in force.
- Civil Society Organisations such as NGOs etc., having proven track record of working in the fields of women's welfare/social welfare/ women's education subject to the condition that such organisation is registered under the Indian Societies Registration Act, 1860 or any relevant State Act;
- The organisation should meet the following criteria:
  - It should be either recognised by the State/UT Administration under any existing scheme/law or should be well-known with the experience of working in the field for at least three years, and its work should be reported to be satisfactory by the State Government/Union Territory Administration concerned.
  - It should ordinarily have been engaged in the field of women's welfare/social welfare/women's education for a minimum period of two years prior to the request for grant-in-aid under the scheme.
  - It should have facilities, resources, personnel and experience to undertake the management of such a project.
  - Its financial position should be sound to take care of expenditure for a few months in case the grant is delayed.
  - It should run the swadhar greh on a no-profit basis.
  - The organisation should have facilities like computers, internet connections etc at swadhar greh.

- Organisation will be given sanction for swadhar greh for a period of five (5) years to begin with. After the expiry of five years period, it will be renewed for a further period of five (5) years each time.

G. Components of the Scheme

- Construction grant for construction of the building will be admissible to State Governments, Municipal Corporations and Panchayati Raj Institutions only. Land for this purpose is to be provided by the implementing agency free of cost.
- Rent for swadhar greh, if runs in a rented building.
- Assistance for recurring and non-recurring expenditure for management of swadhar greh.
- Provision for food, shelter, clothing, medical care, pocket expense for residents and children.
- Provision of counselling, legal-aid, vocational training and guidance.
- Provision of helpline.

H. Pattern of Assistance

The implementing agencies may seek assistance for all the components as mentioned above under the scheme. However, assistance can be sought for a few components provided that the other facilities are available to assist the women in difficult circumstances. Government shall provide following type of financial assistance to the implementing organisations for setting up/running of swadhar greh:

i. **Assistance for Construction:** Government shall grant assistance for construction of rooms/cottages/ huts for the shelter of the residents and common facilities like kitchen, bathroom, training hall, recreation room, dining hall office room etc and infrastructure facilities like water, electricity, approach road, boundary wall etc. The cost of construction would be shared by Central Government and the State Government in the proportion of 75 per cent and 25 per cent respectively. The central Government's share shall be subject to a ceiling of Rs. 1,00,000/- per resident. *Construction grant will be given to State Governments agencies including Women Development Corporation, Municipal Corporations and Panchayati Raj Institutions only.*

ii. **Assistance for Rent:** The amount of rent of the building would be shared between Centre and the implementing organisation in proportion of 90 per cent and 10 per cent respectively subject to a maximum of Rs 25,000/- per month for a swadhar greh intended for 30 residents. It would however, be ensured that the building is not located in high rent areas. Reasonableness of the rent should be certified by the District Collector/State PWD.

***Norms for Residential Space*:** The swadhar greh should provide such residential facilities that would ensure a respectable and dignified standard of living for residents. Accordingly every swadhar greh should provide a residential space of not less than 80 sq. ft. excluding common space and utilities. Besides, every swadhar greh should be properly ventilated with adequate facilities of bathrooms, toilets, and dining hall. Premises for swadhar greh should be clearly defined and no other residential programme should operate in the premises demarcated for swadhar greh.

(Amount in Rupees)

S. No	*Name of the Post*	*No. of Posts*	*Remuneration (Monthly)*	*Remuneration (Yearly)*
1.	Resident Superintendent	1	12000	144000

(Contd.)

(Contd. Table)

S. No	Name of the Post	No. of Posts	Remuneration (Monthly)	Remuneration (Yearly)
2.	Counsellor	1	10000	120000
3.	Office Assistant cum-DEO	1	8000	96000
4.	Multipurpose workers	1	5000	60000
5.	Guard/Watchman	2	10000	120000
	Total	**7**	**45000**	**540000**

iii. **Administration and Management:** The indicative provision of staff for a 30 residents swadhar greh with women helpline would be as under:

iv. **Other Recurring Expenditure:** The following recurring expenditure for the swadhar greh of 30 residents shall be sanctioned.

(Amount in Rupees)

S. No	Particulars	Unit	Expenditure (Monthly)	Expenditure (Yearly)
1.	Expenditure towards food	Per resident	1200	432000#
2.	Expenditure towards clothing	Per resident	------	30000 #
3.	Expenditure towards medicines personal hygiene products etc.	Per resident	200	72000 #
4.	Pocket Money	Per resident	100	36000 #
5.	Expense for Recreational activities	Consolidated		12000 #

(Contd.)

(Contd. Table)

S. No	*Particulars*	*Unit*	*Expenditure (Monthly)*	*Expenditure (Yearly)*
6.	Reimbursement of fees for vocational training under NCVT approved plan and certificate to be issued	Reimbursement of training and test fees as per the norms fixed by the Labour Dept./ NCVT per women	*Rs.1800/- per resident p.a.	27000** (subject to actual)
7.	Contingency including telephone charges	Per home		50000
	Total			**6,59,000**

\# For the women in the age group of 25 to 35 and their children will get all the benefits only for a period of six months and after that they will get the facilities of accommodation only and arrange all their expenses from their own resources.

* Expenditure for Vocational Training has been calculated @ Rs 1800/- per resident for the courses approved by NCVT, training fee for which ranges from Rs 500/- to Rs 2000/- depending upon the duration of training. It is estimated that the average training fee will be Rs 1000/- per resident (after adjusting the available 25 per cent relaxation in training fee for women). After including the test fee of Rs 800/- per woman, the tentative training cost comes to Rs 1800/- per resident.

** It is estimated that fifty per cent of the residents will avail training facilitating in their rehabilitation. The estimated yearly expenditure on vocational training head for a swadhar greh having capacity of 30 women will therefore be Rs 27000/-. The organisation will however be given reimbursement for training fees on actual basis.

Provision for Children: For the children of swadhar greh, expenditure will be given @ 2/3 of the recurring expenditure applicable to women on each head.

Quantum of Periodic Increase in the Financial Assistance:

- Annual increment in the salary of the staff @ five per cent per annum.
- Annual increment in the recurring expenditure @ five per cent per annum.
- An increase up to five per cent in the rent would be considered after every two years subject to the actual.
- A provision of ten per cent increase in the construction cost after every three years from the date of notification of the scheme.
- Implementing agencies that have their own buildings would be entitled for maintenance-cum-upkeep grant of twenty five per cent of the amount of rent of a swadhar greh of equivalent capacity.

v. **Non-Recurring Expenditure**
There would be a provision of one-time non-recurring grant of Rs 5000/- per women for purchase of necessary items including furniture, beds, bedding utensils etc.

vi. From the 12th Five year Plan, twenty five per cent of the costs (ten per cent for North-Eastern States) towards running of swadhar grehs shall be shared by the respective State Governments/UTs Administration.

Duties of the Staff of Swadhar Greh

Resident Superintendent: She will be the overall incharge/administrative head of the swadhar greh and ensures smooth functioning of swadhar greh so that problems of residents of swadhar greh could be sorted out by her.

Counsellor: She will provide counselling to the residents of swadhar greh as well as needy women through telephone. She will also assist Resident Superintendent in managing swadhar greh.

Multi-purpose Workers: These workers will look after various responsibilities of swadhar greh such as accompanying the residents to vocational training programmes, hospital, court and other places as required. They will also arrange general maintenance and the grocery items for the swadhar greh.

Qualification:

Superintendent	-	Post Graduate
Counsellor	-	Masters in Social Work/ Psychology/Sociology
Office Assistant	-	Graduate (with proficiency in Computer operation)
Multi-Purpose Worker	-	Class 12th
Guard/Watchman/ Peon	-	Middle Level

The relaxation in educational qualification would be permissible to the staff of existing homes who have been working for more than five years.

Support Services

Legal Service: The legal assistance requirements of the beneficiaries shall be met through the District Legal Services Authority. Wherever District Legal Service Authority is not available, the implementing organisation will arrange alternative suitable legal assistance.

Vocational Training: Arrangement would be made by the organisation for providing vocational training to the women through the Vocational Training Institute recognised by Directorate General of Employment and Training under the Ministry of Labour and Employment.

Training and examination fee would be reimbursed on submission of the certificate issued by the vocational training institute on successful completion of training. The expenditure incurred by the organisation on the transportation of residents in course of vocational training etc may be met from the contingencies head.

Medical Facilities: Health check–up and medical facilities will be tied up with local civil hospital/CHC/PHC. However, implementing organisation may arrange a part time doctor for swadhar greh and expenditure towards doctor may be met from the 'medical care and personal hygiene head'.

Counselling: The staff proposed under Swadhar Greh scheme will provide the telephonic counselling to the needy women and the expenses towards the telephone calls will be met from the 'Contingency' head of the proposed scheme.

During the course of implementation of the merged scheme, State Governments as well as implementing organisations will establish necessary linkages with other programmes such as Non-Formal Education, Skill Development and other programmes of the States as well as of the Government of India.

All the implementing organisations will coordinate with NACO, State AIDS Control Societies and districts hospitals to take care of the needs of the residents infected/affected by HIV/AIDS.

State Governments will nominate suitable agencies for orientation programme for the functionaries of swadhar grehs to improve the quality of services to be provided in swadhar greh.

I. Sanction of the Proposal

(I) The State Government will send a consolidated proposal containing all the applications of suitable organisations in the prescribed format, complete in all respect duly approved by the State Level Empowered Committee to the Ministry of Women and Child Development, Government of India, Shastri Bhavan, New Delhi.

(II) Each proposal will be scrutinised as per the norms of the scheme and the proposals which fulfill the norms will be placed before the Project Approval Board which will be constituted under the Chairpersonship of Secretary(WCD) with the following composition:

i. Financial Adviser, Ministry of Women and Child Development. – Member

ii. Senior Advisor, Planning Commission. – Member

iii. Joint Secretary of the concerned Bureau in the MWCD. – Member

iv. Director of concerned Division, Ministry of WCD. – Member

v. Director, NIPCCD. – Member

vi. Director, Ministry of HRD. – Member

vii. Director, Ministry of Labour and Employment. – Member

viii. Director, Ministry of Home Affairs. – Member

ix. Director, Ministry of Social Justice and Empowerment . – Member

(III) The PAB shall be the final authority for accepting, reviewing, and sanctioning of proposals for assistance under the scheme.

J. Procedure for Release of Grant for Construction of Swadhar Grehs

The grant for construction cost for new swadhar greh shall be released in three (3) installments, in the ratio of

50:40:10. The one-time grants proposed to be introduced for purchase of furniture and common area facilities may be released with the final installment of ten per cent of the construction cost.

(a) After the proposal is approved, the implementing agency shall submit the building plan approved by the local authority along with the building permission for release of the grant. After that first installment of grant will be released to the implementing agency.

(b) The second installment will be released after the implementing agency has spent the previous installment along with its own proportionate share of cost in the construction of the building. The Request for release of next installment will be accompanied by:

   i) Utilisation Certificate of the previous installment and an up to date consolidated statement of the actual expenditure incurred on execution of the approved plans and estimates, duly certified by a Chartered Accountant/Government Auditor. The expenditure reflected therein should not be below fifty per cent of the approved estimates (in case of request for release of the second installment), and ninety per cent of the approved estimates (in case of release of third installment).

   ii) The implementing agency should furnish a statement indicating up to date physical progress of the construction work to this Ministry regularly at the end of each quarter and the quarterly progress report on the construction work till the building is completed.

(c) The 3rd and final installment will be released on the completion of the construction of the building, along with the one-time grants mentioned above, provided the following documents are produced:

(i) Completion certificate from State PWD/CPWD/ Housing Board to the effect that the building has been completed in accordance with the approved plans and estimates; and

(ii) Consolidated Utilisation Certificate (which would also include Utilisation Certificates of first and second installments clearly and separately indicated) and Statement of Expenditure incurred on the construction of building duly audited by the authorised auditors/Government auditors/ Chartered Accountant.

(iii) Dated photographs of at least the four corners, front elevation, side elevation and one close up showing the name board mentioning that the swadhar greh has been constructed with the financial assistance from the Ministry of Women and Child Development, Government of India.

The detailed guidelines regarding the procedure to be followed for construction grant is given at Appendix-I.

Swadhar Grehs in Rented Premises

Where assistance is sought towards swadhar greh on rent, release shall be made in two equal installments every year. The one-time grant for non-recurring items shall be released with the first installment.

(a) First installment will ordinarily be released along with the sanctioning of the Project. The implementing agency will furnish two colour photographs of the swadhar greh with the name board, mentioning that the building is being run with financial assistance of the Ministry of Women and Child Development, Government of India.

(b) The second and subsequent installment will be released after the implementing agency furnishes proof that it has spent the previous installment for the purpose for which it was granted. Release of the second and subsequent installment shall be accompanied by the following documents:

(i) Utilisation Certificate of the previous installment and an up to date consolidated statement of the actual expenditure incurred

(ii) Inspection Report by the District administration giving the details of general condition of the swadhar greh and facilities provided in the swadhar greh along with the details of present occupancy along with break-up of actual number of children found present at the time of inspection against the approved occupancy of the residents.

In case of subsequent request for continuation of the grant, State Governments will submit consolidated proposal including applications of all the implementing agencies which are running swadhar greh in their States with specific recommendations about the functioning of each and every swadhar greh keeping in view all the aspects of the scheme. PAB will consider all the proposals for continuation of grant. Only after the approval of PAB, further installment of grant will be released to the implementing agencies.

State Governments are required to furnish the consolidated proposal for release of first installment of annual grant by 30th April and by 31st October for the second installment of the respective financial year so that the funds could be released to implementing agencies on time.

The detailed guidelines regarding the procedure to be followed for grant for rented building are provided at Appendix-II.

The guidelines/Instructions for Admission Policy, Services to be provided and Maintenance of Records of the Swadhar Greh is at Appendix-III.

K. Monitoring of Scheme

(i) Monitoring at the District Level

All the swadhar grehs established under the scheme whether newly constructed or running in rented premises or otherwise, would be monitored continuously by the District Administration in order to ensure their smooth functioning, identifying groups and suggesting steps that would lead to their better functioning.

For this purpose, a District Women's Welfare Committee (DWWC) would be constituted in every district to look after the affairs of every swadhar greh in the district. DWWC will conduct need-based assessment in their respective districts and inform State Government about the magnitude of prevalence of such cases so that the proposed swadhar greh could accommodate the estimated destitute women. Further, it would be responsible for providing accreditation, forwarding and recommending proposals, sending recommendations for release of installments of the grant, undertaking periodic monitoring of the functioning of swadhar grehs in their local area, as provided under the scheme and facilitating for generating awareness about the scheme. The DWWC shall be headed by the District Collector/District Magistrate as the case may be, and shall have following as members:

- Chief Medical Officer,
- Superintendent of Police,
- District Social Welfare Officer/Women and Child Development Officer.
- Representative of District Legal Services Authority.
- Noted social worker in the field of women welfare.

- Representative of the Municipal Corporations/ Panchayati Raj Institutions.
- Other eminent persons of the district at the discretion of District Collector.

It should be ensured that at least two members of the DWWC shall be women. The DWWC shall meet at least once in six months or in case an issue arises for immediate resolution.

Each implementing agency will submit the Quarterly Progress Report (QPR) of swadhar greh, list of Rehabilitated Women and list of present women etc in the prescribed format to the DWWC. For second time, applications for continuation of the grant-in-aid following review of the swadhar greh, the DWWC would send its recommendations to the State Government.

(ii) Monitoring at the State Level

The Secretary in–charge of Social Welfare/ Department of Women and Child Development in the State Government/UT Administration shall be the chairperson of the State Level/UT Administration Monitoring Committee for the scheme. The other members of the Committee would be nominated by the Secretary. The Committee at the State Level/UT Administration shall meet at least twice a year and monitor the projects. The continuation of grant to the agency would be based on the satisfactory performance reported by the State Government/UT Administration.

(iii) Monitoring at the Central Level

MWCD shall also review the functioning of the swadhar greh in every five years. Wherever felt necessary, the implementation of the project is got inspected by the officers of the Ministry of WCD.

L. Evaluation of the Scheme

The scheme would be evaluated after three years by an independent agency identified for this purpose. The evaluation would be done to monitor the impact of scheme on the intended beneficiaries as well as identifying the gaps, if any, in the implementation of the scheme and suggest remedies thereof.

M. In Case of Default

(a) In the event of any violation or breach of any provision of the scheme or the implementing agency/swadhar greh ceasing to exist at any time, all assets created out of Government grant shall revert to the Government of India or the amount involved would be recovered as arrears of land revenue from the implementing agency in case of swadhar grehs constructed on public land or under the relevant Rent Control Act in case of other swadhar grehs, or under the Indian Penal Code, as may be applicable.

(b) In addition to this, in the case of any misappropriation of funds by civil society groups/public trusts/cooperatives/corporate bodies, the State Government would initiate criminal proceedings by lodging an FIR against the defaulting implementing agency, and taking strict legal action in order to recover the grant with a penal rate of interest as agreed in the bond to be furnished before the release of grant.

(c) The Government of India through the Ministry or State Departments may be entitled to take over the swadhar greh building and/or assets created by the grant provided under the Scheme, if the implementing agency mis utilises the financial assistance or wrongly use the swadhar greh building for any other purpose.

(d) In case of any minor default (like keeping less residents and reporting higher number, treating badly with the residents, making wrong entry in the book of records and keeping such women who does not cover under the scheme) by the implementing agencies, the PAB of the Ministry on its own or on recommendation of the State Government shall be empowered to deduct up to ten per cent of the sanctioned amount as penalty. For a major default (like siphoning of funds for some other purpose and submission of forged documents), besides the action proposed in the preceding paras, the swadhar greh will be de-recognised and name of the organisation will be listed as a blacklisted organisation in thc Ministry's website. Ministry shall also refuse grants/assistance to an organisation in which the person, who is in the Board of Management of the blacklisted organisation, is also a trustee/ member of the Board of Management.

N. Transitional Provisions

The State Government/UT Administration would undertake a comprehensive review of the all existing shelter homes in the State/UT through District Administration within a period of three months of the notification of the Scheme. The State Government would follow the certain criteria/instructions, included in the Scheme, while furnishing the report for shelter homes. The follow up action to be taken by the Ministry is as under.

State Governments will undertake a comprehensive review of the all existing Swadhar Homes and SSHs with in a time-bound manner through a well-defined mechanism and criteria. The criteria for furnishing the report by State Government would include but not be limited to:

- Location of the Home and need assessment;
- Condition of the building where it is situated and the size of the Home;
- The number of residents existing and could be accommodated within the home in future;
- Strength of the staff and the manner in which the Home is being managed;

- Facilities available to the residents of the Home;
- Number of women got shelter during last five years or since the inception of the home;
- Number of women got rehabilitated during the entire period of functioning of shelter home; and
- Extent the rehabilitation of women.

Ministry will obtain State-wise consolidated proposals for converting those swadhar homes/short stay homes into swadhar greh which are found functioning satisfactorily and need for continuation is justified.

A Project Advisory Board (PAB) will be constituted in the Ministry under the chairpersonship of Secretary, WCD. The PAB will give its approval/sanctions to each proposal submitted by the State Government for setting up/running of swadhar greh;

Proposals for setting up of new swadhar greh for uncovered districts justified with need assessment will also be obtained by State Governments with the recommendation of LEC.

To Raise Awareness in Public

The scheme will be publicised through the State Governments. Each implementing agency will also disseminate information about the swadhar greh to the people though various available modes.

Appendix-I

Procedure to be Followed for Sanctioning of Grant for Construction of Building

State Govt./ UT Administration should submit the application including the followings documents:

Detailed financial estimates of the construction of building, as approved by the PWD/any other competent authority/certified by a registered architect, and giving items-wise details of expenditure.

A copy of site-plan and building plan of the proposed swadhar greh in accordance with the norms prescribed under this scheme, as certified by a registered architect. The building plan approved by the Ministry for the construction of the building should include a certificate from the local Municipal Authorities that its building plan has been approved and construction has been permitted.

Documentary proof of the plot on which the swadhar greh is proposed to be constructed being a public land. Documents of transfer of title/lease deed as signed by the District Collector or any other officer of the Government entitled to do so, shall be submitted along with the application.

Other Conditions to be Followed by the State Govt.

The building would be constructed in accordance with the plan approved by the Government of India. No change in the plan can be made without the prior approval of MWCD, Govt. of India.

However, if any change in the building plans is considered necessary by the implementing agency, subject to the satisfaction of the Ministry, it may be authorised to proceed with the change, intimating full particulars thereof to the Government of India. This is subject to the implementing agency obtaining the approval of the local authority, as required under the relevant building bye-laws and the District Administration. The implementing agency must further ensure that there is no reduction in the living area, built up area or capacity of the swadhar greh.

No additional financial liability will be devolved on the Government of India as a result of the change in building plans, and no cost escalation on this account shall be eligible for further financial assistance under the scheme.

The rates of construction to be adopted in the detailed structural/financial estimates shall not be in excess of the Schedule of Rates of the PWD of the State concerned and a certificate to that effect shall be furnished by the Executive Engineer of State PWD. The Scrutiny Charges Fee levied by State PWD/CPWD would qualify for grant - in-aid under the scheme subject to overall ceiling.

The building shall be completed as soon as possible and in any case not later than 18 months from the date of release of first installment of the grant.

Any unspent portion of the grant shall be refunded to the Government of India at once.

The State Govt./UT Administration shall maintain record of all assets acquired wholly or substantially out of Government Grant. Such assets shall not be disposed off encumbered or utilised for purposes other than those for which grant was given without prior sanction of the Government of India.

Appendix-II

Procedure to be Followed for Sanctioning of Grant for Swadhar Greh in Rented Building

The implementing agencies would submit the application with the followings documents:

i. Valid Registration Certificate and Prospectus of the agency/voluntary organisation/institution or a brief description of its objects and activities;

ii. Constitution of the agency/ organisation/institution;

iii. Constitution of its Board of Management, giving names of members and their PAN Card details;

iv. Annual Reports for the last three years;

v. Copy of the rent agreement as certified by the competent authority;

vi. A copy of the Rent Assessment Certificate duly issued by the State PWD/District Collector/Municipal Authorities;

vii. A blue print of the site plan giving details of the swadhar greh in terms of number of rooms, their size etc.

viii. A statement of full receipts and expenditure of the agency/ organisation/institution for the last three years and a copy of the balance sheet for the last three years certified by authorised auditors/chartered accountant for assessing financial viability of the applicant and sustainability of the swadhar greh.

ix. A certificate of suitability of the proposed premises for use as a swadhar greh from the concerned municipal authority/panchayati raj institution etc.

Appendix-III

Guidelines/Instructions for Admission Policy, Services to be Provided and Maintenance of Records of the Swadhar Greh

When women come to such swadhar greh either on their own or are referred by others, the first step will be to know their social background, the cause of their distress and the problem of adjustment. A specialised interview and case file would be developed by the counsellor (until a standard protocol is developed by MWCD and circulated), to assist her overcome her initial trauma as well as to identify the suitability of services available at swadhar greh as per needs of the victim.

The first series of interviews by the counsellor/ superintendent and the primary stage of diagnosis of the problem are the most vital in deciding the rehabilitation programmes for the women. If on diagnosis, it is found that facilities provided at the swadhar greh are suited to meet the needs of the victim, the applicant may be admitted and provided services for rehabilitation. If it is found that the services offered at the swadhar greh would not meet the problem of the applicant, she should be referred to other suitable institutions in the community, *e.g.*, women victims of trafficking should avail the benefits under Ujjawala scheme.

On arrival, she should be registered in the admission register with details such as name, address, age, details of children (if any), description of the problem and source of reference.

Each case should have a separate file with complete case record, addresses of relatives, referral letters and other letter pertaining to the court case, police etc. A record of assistance provided should also be maintained like meetings held in connection of the case with various authorities, medical check-ups conducted etc. These case files should be updated and open for inspection to any officer of the Government at any time.

The case file should also contain a plan of action for the rehabilitation of each resident and her children (if accompanied) and the steps taken for their rehabilitation.

The information of each and every victim admitted in the swadhar greh should be sent to the nearest police station within 48 hours and an acknowledgement/copy of FIR be kept on record.

A separate case register is to be maintained for the children of beneficiaries, which will reflect the services provided to them including the expenditure incurred on the activities.

If the women brings any valuables with her (gold, silver, jewellery etc). the details should be entered in a register meant for the purpose and counter signed by the Resident Superintendent and the resident. The valuables should be kept in safe custody and handed over to her when she leaves the institution.

Every woman would be provided with a Photo ID-Card till such time as the proposed UID Cards are operationalised.

A medical check-up of every woman would be undertaken within three days of her admission. The arrangement of medical check-up should made by the organisation in the nearest government run hospital/ dispensary. Cases requiring urgent medical attention should be referred to nearest government run hospitals.

In case the resident is known to have contracted HIV/ AIDS or is HIV+, she should be referred to the VCTC centre of the nearest government run hospital for counselling and advice.

Adequate medical facilities including medical kit should be maintained at each swadhar greh. The medical kit should include basic items like antibiotics, burn creams, tape, bandages, strips for wound closure and management, scissors etc.

There should be facilities for recreation and group activities. Facilities for indoor and outdoor games should be provided. They should be taken out for cultural shows, outings, movies, picnics and exhibitions etc at least once a month. The swadhar greh should also celebrate different religious festivals, Republic Day, Independence Day and the birthdays of the children with active involvement of residents. Each swadhar greh should have a provision of television for residents.

The implementing agency would be responsible for the provision of vocational training of the residents through Skill Development Initiative (SDI) scheme of Ministry of Labour and Employment. The Ministry would reimburse the amount of fees as per the actual expenditure incurred in the training course.

4

Demographic Profile of Selected States

Uttar Pradesh

The history of Uttar Pradesh is very ancient and interesting. It is recognised in the later Vedic age as Brahmarshi Desha or Madhya Desha. Many great sages of the Vedic time like Bharadwaja, Gautam, Yagyavalkya, Vasishtha, Vishwamitra and Valmiki flourished in this state. Several sacred books of the Aryans were also composed here. Two great epics of India– Ramayana and Mahabharata, appear to have been inspired by Uttar Pradesh.

In the sixth century B.C., Uttar Pradesh was associated with two new religions – Jainism and Buddhism. It was at Sarnath that Buddha preached his first sermon and laid the foundations of his order and it was in Kushinagar in Uttar Pradesh where Buddha breathed his last. Several centres in Uttar Pradesh like Ayodhya, Prayag, Varanasi and Mathura became reputed centres of learning. In the medieval period of Uttar Pradesh was under Muslim rule and led the way to new synthesis of Hindu and Islamic cultures. Ramananda and his Muslim disciple Kabir, Tulsidas, Surdas and many other intellectuals contributed to the growth of Hindi and other languages.

Uttar Pradesh preserved its intellectual excellency even under the British administration. The British combined Agra and Oudh into the one province and called it United Provinces of Agra and Oudh. The name was shortened to the United Provinces in 1935. In January, 1950, the United Provinces was renamed as Uttar Pradesh.

The earliest events which can safely be called historical are connected with the life of Gautam Buddha. The Sinhalese traditions place Gautam's death in 543 B.C., while European scholars have suggested various dates between 477 and 370 B.C. It is certain that he spent much of his life in the eastern districts, and the remains of stupas, monasteries and other relics testify to the extent to which his doctrines were held in all parts of the Provinces as well as beyond their limits. A suggestion has recently been made that Buddhism was a regular development of religious thought among the people of Magadha and not merely a revolt against the growth of Brahmanism in Madhya Desha, as is commonly supposed. As a religious system, it appears to have maintained its position till the fourth century A.D. when a revival of Hinduism took place under the Guptas. The accounts of the Chinese pilgrims in the fifth and seventh centuries A.D. show that Buddhism was then fast waning, and the latest memorial of it as a living faith is an inscription of the twelfth or thirteenth century found in Gonda district.

The first point of contact with Western history comes in the fourth century B.C., with Alexander's invasion and the subsequent relations of Seleucus Nicator with Sandrocottus, who is identified with Chandragupta Maurya of the Puranic annals. Chandragupta's kingdom, the first organised empire in India of which we have historical record, extended after the withdrawal of

Seleucus, from the Hindukush to the Bay of Bengal, with its capital at Patna. The grandson of Chandragupta was Asoka, the first great Buddhist emperor, whose pious edicts have been found on pillars and rocks in many part of India. Three of his inscriptions are known in these provinces, on pillars at Allahabad and Benares and on a rock at Kalsi in Dehradun. The last mentions by name of contemporary kings of Syria, Egypt, Macedonia, Cyrene and Epirus and thus fixes the date of Asoka's coronation at 270 or 269 B.C. These inscriptions, and the fragments which have survived from writings of Megasthenese, the ambassador of Seleucus at the court of Patna, show a highly developed system of government.

If the chronology of the Puranas is to be accepted, the Mauryan dynasty came to an end about 188 or 178 B.C., and was succeeded by the Sunga, but there is no independent confirmation of this. Numismatic evidence points to the conclusion that about his time parts of at least four kingdoms were included in the provinces, corresponding to the ancient Surasena (round Mathura), North Panchala (Rohilkhand), Kosala (round Ayodhya), and a tract south of Allahabad which may have been the kingdom of Kosambhi. From their coins the kings of Panchala and Mathura appear to have been Hindus, while the symbols on the coins of Ayodhya and Kosambhi are often Buddhist.

The Provinces had been free from foreign invaders for about four hundred years, when in 1018, Mahmud of Ghazni crossed the Yamuna, and took Bulandshahr, the rich city of Mathura with its temples full of jewels and gold, and Kannauj. This expedition and two more in 1021 and 1023 directed against Kannauj, Gwalior and Kalingar were mere raids, in which plunder rather than conquest was the aim.

Early in the sixteenth century the capital was moved from Delhi to Agra, which was to become a great city under the Mongols or Mughals, who now appeared again. In 1526, Babar defeated the Afghan king, Ibrahim at Panipat but found himself in difficulties at Agra. On the west, the Rajputs were united under the Rana of Udaipur, while on the east, the Afghans were threatening an attack from Kannauj. The crown prince, Humayun made a successful raid as far as Jaunpur and Ghazipur and Babar gained a great victory over the Rajputs near Fatehpur Sikri.

After the death of Akbar in 1605 at Agra, his son succeeded as Jahangir. In 1623 Kurram, another son of the emperor, rebelled and advanced towards Mathura, but was driven back to Central India. On Jahangir's death at Lahore in 1627, Kurrum hastened to Agra and obtained the throne under the name of Shah Jahan. Early in his reign the Bundelas, who had been turbulent throughout Akbar's life, but had been friendly to Jahangir broke out and several expeditions were sent against them. Aurangzeb entered Agra in 1658 and he formally assumed the throne at Lahore.

After the death of Aurangzeb in 1707, he left a will advising his three sons to divide the empire. The second son, Azam refused to accept the division and fell in battle at Jajau in Agra, fighting the eldest brother Muazzam, who became the emperor under the title of Shah Alam Bahadur.

At the commencement of the nineteenth century, the British thus held only the present Benares division (except South Mirzapur) and the fort of Allahabad. In 1801, when Rohilkhand and other parts of the Oudh territory were in a state of anarchy, and a grandson of Ahmad Shah Durrani was threatening to invade India, Saadat Ali, Nawab of Oudh, in return for a guarantee of protection , made over to the British the so-called 'Ceded Provinces', which included the present Gorakhpur and Rohilkhand divisions, with the districts of Allahabad, Fatehpur, Kanpur, Etawah,

Mainpuri, Etah, the south of Mirzapur, and the Tarai parganas of the Kumaun division.

The early Muhammadans have left many memorials in the shape of mosques, idgahs and tombs. The oldest among these are some buildings constructed at Budaun by the emperor Altamsh in the beginning of the thirteenth century. The finest specimens are, however, the great mosques at Jaunpur, built two hundred years later by the Sharki kings, which are particularly striking for their huge facades, recalling the propylons of Egypt.

During the sixteenth and seventeenth centuries, the emperors, Akbar, Jahangir, and Shah Jahan spent large sums on the adornment of the royal residences at Fatehpur Sikri and Agra, where stately palaces, magnificent tombs and mosques still recall the memories of the great Mughals. Much has been done within the last few years to repair and preserve these valuable monuments. In the eighteenth century, the type of architecture deteriorated, though buildings of some beauty were built by the Rohillas and the early Nawabs of Oudh.

Location

Uttar Pradesh is truly the heart land of India situated in Northern India and shares its border with Himachal, Punjab, Delhi, Madhya Pradesh, Bihar and international border with Nepal. It lies between latitude of 24 degrees to 31 degrees and longitude of 77 degrees to 54 degrees.

Area

Uttar Pradesh has an area of 2.94 million square kilometer. Area-wise it is fourth largest state.

Physiography

Uttar Pradesh can be divided into three distinct regions:

- The Himalayan region in the north;

- The Gangetic plain in the centre;
- The Vindhya hills and Plateau in the south.

The transitional belt running along the entire length of the state is called the 'terai' and 'bhabhar' areas. The main crops are wheat, rice and sugarcane.

The Gangetic plain is watered by the Yamuna, the Ganga and its major tributaries, the Ramganga, the Gomti, the Ghaghra and Gandak. The whole plain is alluvial and very fertile. The chief crops cultivated here are rice, wheat, millets, gram and barley. Sugarcane is the chief cash crop of the region. The southern fringe of the Gangetic plain is demarcated by the Vindhya hills and plateau. It has four distinct kinds of soil, two of which are agriculturally difficult to manage. They are black cotton soil.

Rainfall is scanty and erratic and water resources are scarce. Dry farming is practiced on a large scale.

Climate

The climate of the state is tropically monsoon, but variations exist because of difference in altitudes. The Himalayan region is cold. The average temperature varies in the plains from 3-4^{0}C in January to 43-45^{0}C in May and June. There are three distinct seasons – the Cold season from October to February, summer from March to mid-June and the rainy season from June to September. The Himalayan region has about 100-200 cm of rainfall.

Floods are a recurring problem of the states causing damage to crops, life and property. There are occasional cloud bursts adding to the misery of the people. The proneness is ascribed to the heavy rainfall, low flat country, high sub-soil water level and the silting of beds which causes river levels to rise. Poor drainage is caused by obstruction of roads, railways, canals, new built-up areas.

Soil

The Valley area has fertile and rich soil. There is an intensive cultivation on terraced hill slopes. The higher altitudes are suitable for sub-tropical and temperate fruit culture. The Siwalik range, which forms the southern foot hills of the Himalayas, slopes down into a boulder bed called 'bhadhar'.

Hills

The prominent peaks in the hill region include Banarpunch, Mount Kamety, Trishul, Dunagiri, Nanda Devi, Badrinath and Kedarnath. The hill areas are sparsely populated. Due to the excessive nature of the terrain, soil is subject to heavy erosion. Cultivation is done

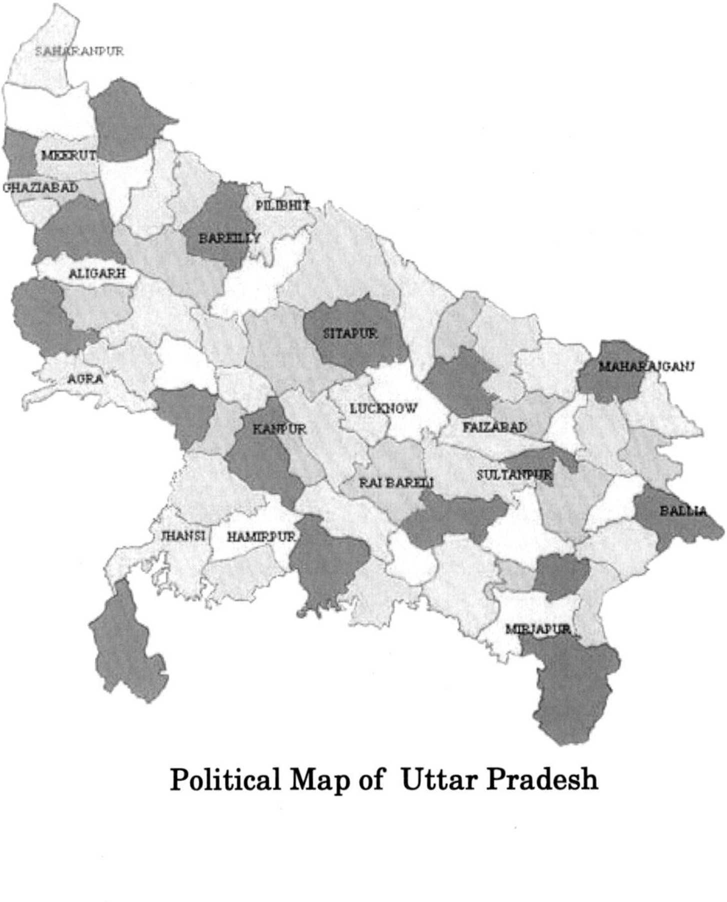

Political Map of Uttar Pradesh

under intensive soil. Irrigation facilities are deficient and only a small fraction of the total area is under artificial irrigation.

Rivers

The major rivers are the Ganga, Yamuna, Gomti, Ghaghra, Rapti, Sarda and Ramganga.

Population of Uttar Pradesh

Despite carving out a separate state of Uttaranchal from Uttar Pradesh, the state still way ahead of all states and Union territories in terms of population. Its population as on 1st March 2011 stood at 199,581,477 as per the provisional results of the Census of India 2011.

According to Census of India, 2011 the total population stood at 199,581,477 out of which total males are 104,596,415 and total females were 94,985,062. The sex ratio (*i.e.* the number of females per thousand males) of population is recorded as 908, which was improved from 898 worked out during the previous census.

The population of the state rose by 20.09 per cent during the decade 2001–2011. The growth of males and females in percentage terms are 19.45 per cent and 20.80 per cent respectively. Further if we look at population between zero to six years, we find that total male child in this age group are 15,653,175 and total female child are 14,075,060, whereas total population of children between

Table – 4.1: Population 2011

Category	*Number*
Persons	199,581,477
Males	104,596,415
Females	94,985,062
Sex Ratio	908

this age group stood at 29,728,238 which is 14.90 per cent of the total population.

Table – 4.2: Decadal Growth 2001– 2011

Category	*Percentage*
Persons	(+) 20.09
Males	(+) 19.45
Females	(+) 20.80

Table – 4.3: Population (0 – 6 Years), 2011

Category	*Number*
Persons	29,728,238
Males	15,653,175
Females	14,075,060
Sex Ratio	899

Table – 4.4: Percentage of Population (0–6) to Total Population

Category	*Percentage*
Persons	14.90
Males	14.97
Females	14.82

The central fact of the social order in Uttar Pradesh is the existence of the caste system among the Hindus, who constitute the vast majority of the population.

A separate sub-caste, which is lower than the full-blodded Brahmins in hierarchy but higher than the Kshatriyas, thereby came into existence, known as Bhumihars. Several others of Khatris and Bishnois can be cited. These arose out of an intermixture of blood and other factors.

The rigid caste attitudes in the past and the social and political tensions have resulted in the growth of large settlements of particular castes in compact regions in Uttar Pradesh. Thus, there are large pockets of Ahirs, Gujjars, Kurmis, Bhumihars, and so on in different parts. The scheduled castes and the Harijans have their own settlement everywhere. The village leadership is in the hands of upper castes while in the urban areas, the trading class (Vaishyas) with plenty of money to spend, is well-knit community and has a large say in direction of affairs.

The Muslims are not evenly distributed over the state. They are found in western division of Meerut, Agra and Rohilkhand and in the eastern districts in terai area in Gonda and Baharaich, in Azamgarh, Jaunpur and Ghazipur.

The fertile plains of Uttar Pradesh offered an ideal habitat for the early Muslim settlers, who came in the wake of the establishment of Turkish rule in India. The hostility was confined mainly within the ruling classes – The Rajas, Rawats, Rais and the original village echelons and the muqtis and their subordinates. Years before the Ghurid conquest of northern India, the Muslims had settled in Badaun, Bahraich, Kannauj, Unnao and Bilgram. Muslim concentration in towns was primarily due to their socio-political organisations, their exclusive racial and religious complexion. Muslims have always had an influential upper class consisting of Nawabs, Rajas and Chaudhries because of their historical antecedents.

The middle class, comparatively thin among Muslims, is engaged in the traditional trades like leather, timber (in the terai area), tobacco and perfume (in Lucknow). There is only a sprinkling of Muslims in the services and professions. Commerce and trade was not a Muslim forte.

A part of Uttar Pradesh mainly tribal areas with the following districts such as Dehradun, Uttarkashi, Tehri Garhwal, Rudraprayag, Chamoli, Hardwar, Pauri Garhwal, Bageshwar, Pithoragarh, Almora, Nainital, Champawat and Udham Singh Nagar has been formed into a new state Uttaranchal. So, part of the tribal population is now in the state of Uttaranchal.

The population of the tribal communities in the state is not large. They constitute the weakest section of the society and form distinct ethnic groups which have preserved their own separate culture identities in their original environment despite the ravages of time.

Uttar Pradesh's greatest gifts to humanity are the two epics, the *'Ramayana'* and the 'Mahabharata'. From the epic age, the territory of Uttar Pradesh being watered by several fresh streams of culture, the two most significant being those generated by the teachings of the Buddha and Mahavira, the 24th Jain Tirthankar.

Karnataka

The name Karnataka is derived from 'Karunadu', literally, lofty land. As much of Karnataka is high plateau land, the name is fully justified. The history of Karnataka goes back to the period of the epics, the capital of Bali and Sugreeva, 'monkey kings' of the Ramayana, is said to have been Hampi in Bellary district. Vatapi, associated with the sage Agastya, is obviously Badami in Bijapur district.

During British rule, the Karnataka area was distributed among the Princely States of Mysore, Hyderabad, and the British provinces of Bombay and Madras and the small principality of Coorg.

The formation of the present State represented the fulfillment of the age-old aspirations of Kannada-speaking people to come together in a single state. The old Kingdom of Mysore formed the nucleus of the new state. Under the

States Reorganisation Act, the Kingdom of Mysore gathered around the districts of Kanara, Bijapur, Dharwar and the major portion of Belgaum district in the Gulbarga, Raichur and Bidar districts, from the princely State of Hyderabad, Dakshina Kannada district (excluding Kasargod Taluk) from the old Madras Presidency and the whole of the 'Part C' State of Coorg.

Location

Karnataka in South-West India is the country's eighth largest state, situated on a table land where the Western and Eastern Ghat ranges converge into the Nilgiri hill complex, the state of Karnataka is confined roughly within 11.5 degrees North and 18.5 degrees North latitudes and 74 degrees East and 78.5 degrees East longitude.

The state is bounded by Maharashtra and Goa states in the North and North-West; by the Arabian Sea in the West; by Kerala and Tamil Nadu states in the South and by the state of Andhra Pradesh in the East. The state extends to about 750km from North to South and about 400km from East to West, and covers an area of about 1,91,791 sq. km.

Karnataka has representatives of all types of variations in topography – high mountains, plateaus, residual hills and coastal plains. The state is enclosed mainly of plateau which has higher elevation of 600 to 900 metres above mean sea level. The entire landscape is undulating, broken up by mountains and deep ravines. Plain land of elevation less than 300 metres above mean sea level is to be found only in narrow coastal belt, facing the Arabian Sea.

There are quite a few high peaks both in Western and Eastern Ghat systems with altitudes more than 1,500 metres. A series of cross-sections drawn from west to east across the Western Ghat generally exhibit, a narrow coastal plain followed to the east by small and short plateaus at different altitudes, then suddenly rising upto great heights.

Then follows the gentle east and east-north-west sloping plateau. Among the tallest peaks of Karnataka are the Mullayyana Giri (1,925m), Bababudaniri (Chandradrona Parvata 1,894m) and the Kuderemukh (1,895m) all in Chikmagalur Dt. and the Pushpagiri (1,908m) in Kodagu Dt. There are a dozen peaks which rise above the height of 1,500 metres.

Area

Karnataka means beautiful land with a magnificent coastline, lush forest, peaks. Situated on the Deccan Plateau the state stretches 760km from North to South and 420km from West to East with a total geographical area of 192,000km.

Physiography

Physiographically, Karnataka state forms part of two well-defined macro regions of Indian Union; the Deccan Plateau and the Coastal plains and Islands. The State has four physiographic regions:

1. *Northern Karnataka Plateau*

Northern Karnataka Plateau comprises the districts of Belgaum, Bidar, Bijapur and Gulbarga and is largely composed of the Deccan Trap. It represents a monotonous, treeless extensive plateau landscape with a general elevation of 300 to 600 metres from the mean sea level. However, the river plains of the Krishna, the Bhima, the Ghataprabha and the Malaprabha with the intervening watersheds, the step like landscapes, lateritic scarpments, residual hills and ridges break the monotony of this extensive plateau. The general slope is towards the east. This region is largely covered with rich black cotton soils.

2. *Central Karnataka Plateau*

Central Karnataka Plateau covers the districts of Bellary, Chikmagalur, Chitradurga, Dharwad, Raichur and Shimoga. The region represents the transitional surface between the Northern Karnataka Plateau of

Deccan Trap and southern Karnataka Plateau with relatively higher surface. By and large, this region represents the area of Tungabhadra basin. The general elevation varies between 450 and 700 metres. The general slope of this region is towards the east.

3. *Southern Karnataka Plateau*

The Sourthern Karnataka Plateau covers the districts of Bangalore, Bangalore Rural, Hassan, Kodagu, Kolar, Mandya, Mysore and Tumkur. This region largely covers the area of the Cauvery river basin lying in Karnataka. It is bounded by 600 metres contour and is characterised by a higher degree of slope. In the west and south, it is enclosed by the ranges of Western Ghats and the northern part is an interrupted but clearly identifiable high plateau.

In the east, the valleys of the Cauvery and its tributaries open out to form undulating plains. The general elevation of the region varies from 600 to 900 metres. However, residual heights of 1,500 to 1,750 metres are found in the Biligirirangan hills of Mysore district and the Brahmagiri range of Kodagu district.

4. *Karnataka Coastal Region*

The Karnataka Coastal Region, which extends between the Western Ghats, edge of the Karnataka Plateau in the east and the Arabian Sea in the West, covers Dakshina Kannada and Uttara Kannada districts. This region is traversed by several ridges and spurs of Western Ghats. It has difficult terrain full of rivers, creeks, water falls, peaks and ranges of hills. The coastal region consists of two broad physical units, the plains and the Western Ghats.

The Coastal plains, represent a narrow stretch of estuarine and marine plains. The abrupt rise at the eastern flanks forms the Western Ghats. The northern parts of the ghats are of lower elevation (450–600 meters) as compared to Southern parts (900 to 1,500 metres). The

Coastal belt with an average width of 50 to 80km covers a distance of about 267km. from north to south.

Climate

The State enjoys three main types of climates. [for meteorological purposes, the State has been divided into three sub-divisions namely; (a) Coastal Karnataka (Dakshina Kannada and Uttara Kannada districts); (b) North Interior Karnataka (Belgaum, Bidar, Bijapur, Dharwad, Gulbarga and Raichur districts), and (c) South Interior Karnataka (the remaining districts of Bangalore Rural, Bangalore, Bellary, Chikmagalur, Chitradurga, Kodagu, Hassan, Kolar, Mysore, Mandya, Shimoga and Tumkur districts).

The tropical monsoon climate covers the entire coastal belt and adjoining areas. The climate in this region is hot with excessive rainfall during the monsoon season *i.e.*, June to September. The Southern half of the state experiences hot, seasonally dry tropical savanna climate while most of the northern half experiences hot, semi–arid, tropical steppe type of climate. The climate of the state varies with the seasons.

The winter season from January to February is followed by summer season from March to May. The period from October to December forms the post–monsoon season. The period from October to March, covering the post-monsoon and winter seasons, is generally pleasant over the entire state except during a few spells of rain associated with north-east monsoon which affects the south-eastern parts of the State during October to December.

The months April and May are hot, very dry and generally uncomfortable. Weather tends to be oppressive during June due to high humidity and temperature. The next three months (July, August and September) are somewhat comfortable due to reduced day temperature although the humidities continue to be very high.

Bangalore is the Capital city of Karnataka. Other main city/towns are Mangalore, Raichur, Dharwad, Bellary, Hassan, and Chickmagalur.

Soil

Karnataka Light Soils (KLS)

The light soils located in Mysore, Hassan, Shimoga, Coorg and Chitradurga districts constitute the light soils of Karnataka. The area is also called as Transitional Zone with light soils and abundant rainfall suitable for tobacco cultivation. The crop is planted in the last week of April–May and harvested in July-August. The yields per hectare are around 1000 kgs. The varieties suitable are Special FCV, Bhavya, Swarna. The tobacco produced is light to medium bodied, lemon orange in colour, soft in nature, open grained. EEC countries and some African and Middle East countries mostly prefer this variety of tobacco.

Hills

The Sahyadris mountain range run from Belgaum in the north to Mysore in the south. They form a triangular area in conjunction with the Eastern Ghats. The Ghats are only 305 to 610 meters in height in the middle but towards the south, they are quite tall and rise to a height of 1830 meters above sea level. It is here that the Nilgiris overlap the Ghats and at places, they rise to 2440 meters. Naturally, at that height there are wooded areas and evergreen valleys, deep gorges, and pleasant plateaus. They lend themselves to the growth of plantations of different kinds which yield coffee, tea, areca nut, cashew nut and cardamom.

Rivers

The Kalinadi, the Gangavathi Bedti, the Tadri, and the Sharavati are the prominent rivers of North Karnataka. Sharavati is the shortest river and is famous for the mighty Jog Falls, the site of the hydel projects. All these rivers are west flowing and some of them are torrential streams which are in full flow in the monsoon.

Most of the major rivers of the state have their origin in the Ghats and flow eastwards towards the Bay of Bengal, through Andhra Pradesh or Tamil Nadu, Krishna with its tributaries like the Bhima and Ghataprabha and Tungabhadra is among these mighty rivers. The Kaveri river in the southern part of the state, which has its origin on Brahma Giri in Coorg, with its tributaries like the Shimsha, Hemavati, Kapila and others enters Tamil Nadu and is a major source of irrigation both in Karnataka and Tamil Nadu. It is a river of discord between the two states because of the great demand on its waters for the farmers in each of the two states and the matter often reaches emotional where politicians take over. The rivers Polar and Pennar in the eastern parts of the state are among the other important rivers.

The Krishna which originates in Maharashtra, is also a cause of dissension between Karnataka and Andhra Pradesh. The coast has several ports. Ports like Karwa, Ankola, Honavar and Bhatkal are situated at the mouth of the rivers where they fall into the Arabian Sea. Mangalore and Malpe are important ports in the southern part of the state and the river of significance is the Netravathi. In ancient times, these ports provided India's contacts, commercial and cultural with far way and near to Egypt and Sumeria.

According to census of India, 2011 the total population of Karnataka stood at 61,130,704 out of which total males are 31,057,742 and total females are 30,072,962. The sex ratio (*i.e.* the number of females per thousand males) of population is recorded as 968.

The population of the state rose by 15.67 per cent during the decade 2001-2011. The growth of males and females in percentage terms are 15.46 per cent and 15.88 per cent respectively. Further, if we look at population between zero to six years, we find that total male child in this age group are 35,27,844 and total female child are 33,27,957 whereas total population of children between this age group stood at 68,55,801 which is 11.21 per cent of the total population.

Table – 4.5: Population 2011

Category	*Number*
Persons	61,130,704
Males	31,057,742
Females	30,072,962
Sex Ratio	968

Table – 4.6: Decadal Growth 2001– 2011

Category	*Percentage*
Persons	(+) 15.67
Males	(+) 15.46
Females	(+) 15.88

Table – 4.7: Population (0 – 6 Years), 2011

Category	*Number*
Persons	68,55,801
Males	35,27,844
Females	33,27,957
Sex Ratio	943

Table – 4.8: Percentage of Population (0–6) to Total Population

Category	*Percentage*
Persons	11.21
Males	11.36
Females	11.07

5

Socio-Economic Status of Universe

The appreciation of any study depends upon the presentation of situation analysis of the sample. For the purpose, the research team collected relevant data to depict social, economic, educational and cultural aspects of the sample. The focus of the study is on empowerment of destitute women through Swadhar Shelter homes in Uttar Pradesh and Karnataka states.

A. Age Distribution

Age plays a vital role in any study where maturity and experience reflects their attitude and behaviour. For the purpose, the total 438 sample is divided into six age categories *i.e.* less than 20, 21 to 30, 31 to 40, 41 to 50, 51 to 60 and more than 60 years. In Uttar Pradesh, there is no respondent upto age of 30 years, while 15.5 per cent and 47.7 per cent respondents belong to less than 20 years and 21 to 30 years age in Karnataka respectively. Majority 60.55 per cent destitute women are above than 60 years in Uttar Pradesh. There is contrast in Karnataka where maximum 47.7 per cent women are between 21 to 30 years of age. The table – 4.01 depicts that women in Uttar Pradesh have more patience in comparison to Karnataka in their respective age group.

Table – 5.1 : Age of Respondents

State	*Age Group (years)*						
	< 20	*21 – 30*	*31 – 40*	*41 – 50*	*51 – 60*	*60 +*	*Total*
Uttar Pradesh	–	–	4 (1.84)	17 (7.79)	65 (29.82)	132 (60.55)	218 (100.0)
Karnataka	34 (7.76)	105 (23.97)	63 (28.6)	18 (8.2)	–	–	220 (100.0)
Total	34 (7.76)	105 (23.97)	67 (15.30)	35 (7.99)	65 (14.84)	132 (30.14)	438 (100.0)

(*Note*: Figures in brackets show percentage)

In Uttar Pradesh more than fifty per cent of the sample has more and more resistance power to accommodate themselves in the family while in Karnataka mostly 47.7 per cent women have less perseverance of any sort of problem with their family. There is special feature that all destitute women in Karnataka are upto fity years of age.

B. Marital Status

Marriage is the natural phenomenon of society. Table – 5.2 reveals that majority of destitute women *i.e.* 86.7 per cent are widow in Uttar Pradesh. It means that after the death of husband they are not being properly cared by their children and other family members so they feel neglected and isolated in family. Mostly 44.09 per cent married women in Karnataka are residing in homes. Overall 49.32 per cent widows represent the sample.

C. Educational Background

To analyse the educational background, the whole sample has been classified into eight categories *viz.,* Illiterate, Literate, Primary, Junior High School, High School, Intermediate, Graduate and Others (Table – 5.3). Uttar Pradesh depicts 44.03 per cent women are illiterate while Karnataka constitutes 36.81 per cent. Education is very much important factor for the betterment of the society as well as individual. It opens the horizon and controls the parochial views and also generates the level of tolerance.

D. Occupation of Respondents

Occupation has been defined in terms of domestic service, labour, private service and others. In Uttar Pradesh, 38.07 per cent respondents are labourers while in Karnataka 19.09 per cent are labourers which is just half of that of Uttar Pradesh. 51.81 per cent women in Karnataka respondents occupation is other type, means they are involved in mixed kind of occupation or intended to work according to the requirements (Table – 5. 4).

Table – 5.2: Marital Status of Respondents

State	*Married*	*Unmarried*	*Divorcee*	*Widow*	*Separated*	*Total*
Uttar Pradesh	13 (5.9)	9 (4.1)	3 (1.4)	189 (86.7)	4 (1.9)	218 (100.0)
Karnataka	97 (44.09)	68 (30.9)	12 (5.46)	27 (12.27)	16 (7.28)	220 (100.0)
Total	110 (25.11)	77 (17.58)	15 (3.42)	216 (49.32)	20 (4.57)	438 (100.0)

(*Note:* Figures in brackets show percentage)

Table – 5.3: Educational Background

State	*Illite.*	*Liter.*	*Prima.*	*Jr. H. Sch.*	*High Sch.*	*Inter*	*Grad.*	*Others*	*Total*
Uttar Pradesh	96 (44.03)	40 (18.36)	10 (4.59)	50 (22.94)	–	–	11 (5.04)	11 (5.04)	218 (100.0)
Karnataka	81 (36.81)	12 (5.45)	48 (21.81)	18 (8.2)	43 (19.55)	2 (.91)	14 (6.36)	2 (.91)	220 (100.0)
Total	**177 (40.41)**	**52 (11.86)**	**58 (13.24)**	**68 (15.56)**	**43 (9.81)**	**2 (.46)**	**25 (5.7)**	**13 (2.96)**	**438 (100.0)**

(*Note:* Figures in brackets show percentage)

Table – 5.4 : Occupation of Respondents

State	*Domestic Service*	*Labour*	*Private Service*	*Others*	*Total*
Uttar Pradesh	37 (16.97)	83 (38.07)	40 (18.35)	58 (26.61)	218 (100.0)
Karnataka	32 (14.55)	42 (19.09)	32 (14.55)	114 (51.81)	220 (100.0)
Total	**69 (15.75)**	**125 (28.53)**	**72 (16.45)**	**172 (39.27)**	**438 (100.0)**

(*Note:* Figures in brackets show percentage)

E. Living Parents

Parents are supposed to be known as backbone for their children in all aspects of development. Table – 5.5 reveals that 75.23 per cent respondents have lost their parents. Only 21 per cent respondents are blessed by their parents in Uttar Pradesh. But 52.72 per cent respondents of Karnataka still enjoy their parents which is just more than fifty per cent of the total Karnataka sample. In comparison to Uttar Pradesh, 47.28 per cent inmates of the home in Karnataka have lost their parents.

Table – 5.5: Living Status of Parents of Respondents

State	*Yes*	*No*	*No Response*	*Total*
Uttar Pradesh	46 (21.0)	164 (75.23)	8 (3.67)	218 (100.0)
Karnataka	116 (52.72)	104 (47.28)	–	220 (100.0)
Total	**162 (37.0)**	**268 (61.2)**	**8 (1.8)**	**438 (100.0)**

(*Note:* Figures in brackets show percentage)

F. Ecological Background of Respondents

Occupancy in home is categorically defined in three groups *i.e.*, urban, semi–urban and rural. In Uttar

Pradesh, 57.34 per cent occupants belong to semi-urban area or fringe area, 27.53 per cent women are from urban areas. In Karnataka, 56.36 per cent are from rural areas. It shows that women of rural society in Karnataka have much more problems than that of Uttar Pradesh (Table – 5.6) whereas in urban society situation is vice-versa.

Table – 5.6: Ecological Background of Respondents

State	*Urban*	*Semi-Urban*	*Rural*	*Total*
Uttar Pradesh	60 (27.53)	125 (57.34)	33 (15.13)	218 (100.0)
Karnataka	68 (30.91)	28 (12.73)	124 (56.36)	220 (100.0)
Total	**128** **(29.2)**	**153** **(34.9)**	**157** **(35.9)**	**438** **(100.0)**

(Note : Figures in brackets show percentage)

G. Religion of Respondents

In Uttar Pradesh, Hundred per cent women belong to Hindu religion, while in Karnataka 86.37 per cent Hindu women are there. Rest 5.45 per cent and 8.18 per cent women are from Muslim and Christian community respectively (Table–5.7).

Table – 5.7: Religion of Respondents

State	*Hindu*	*Muslim*	*Christian*	*Sikh*	*Total*
Uttar Pradesh	218 (100.0)	–	–	–	218 (100.0)
Karnataka	190 (86.37)	12 (5.45)	18 (8.18)	–	220 (100.0)
Total	**408** **(93.15)**	**12** **(2.75)**	**18** **(4.1)**	**–**	**438** **(100.0)**

(*Note:* Figures in brackets show percentage)

H. Social Group (Caste) of Respondents

There is no caste discrimination in homes. But for the study purpose, investigator tried to acknowledge the social group too. As per the Constitution, there are mainly four classification of caste *i.e.*, general, scheduled caste, scheduled tribe and other backward castes. Despite differences, harmony, honesty, love, caring etc. has no caste barrier. First of all they all are human beings and have their own feelings, sentiments, mind-set etc. Table – 5.8 depicts that 56.42 per cent women are from general category in Uttar Pradesh, while in Karnataka 40.91 per cent OBC destitute are present.

Table – 5.8: Social Sub-Group (Caste) of Respondents

State	*General*	*OBC*	*SC*	*ST*	*Total*
Uttar Pradesh	123 (56.42)	54 (24.77)	41 (18.81)	–	218 (100.0)
Karnataka	70 (31.81)	90 (40.91)	50 (22.73)	10 (4.55)	220 (100.0)
Total	**193** **(44.07)**	**144** **(32.88)**	**91** **(20.77)**	**10** **(2.28)**	**438** **(100.0)**

(*Note* : Figures in brackets show percentage)

I. Type of Family of Respondents

Indian society is based on bondings and relationship among family members. Nowadays, it has lost its glory.

Table – 5.9: Type of Family of Respondents

State	*Joint*	*Nuclear*	*Total*
Uttar Pradesh	140 (64.22)	78 (35.78)	218 (100.0)
Karnataka	53 (24.09)	167 (75.91)	220 (100.0)
Total	**193** **(44.06)**	**245** **(55.94)**	**438** **(100.0)**

(*Note* : Figures in brackets show percentage)

Table – 5.10: Family Occupation of Respondents

State	*Business*	*Self-Employed*	*Service*	*Labour*	*Agricul.*	*Others*	*Total*
Uttar Pradesh	46 (21.1)	39 (17.89)	28 (12.85)	55 (25.23)	17 (7.79)	33 (15.14)	218 (100.0)
Karnataka	17 (7.73)	10 (4.54)	10 (4.54)	120 (54.55)	48 (21.82)	15 (6.82)	220 (100.0)
Total	63 (14.38)	49 (11.19)	38 (8.68)	175 (39.95)	65 (14.84)	48 (10.96)	438 (100.0)

(*Note* : Figures in brackets show percentage)

Table – 5.11: Annual Family Income of Respondents

State	*Nil*	*Upto 2000*	*2000 – 5000*	*5000 – 8000*	*8000 – 11000*	*11000 above*	*Total*
Uttar Pradesh	33 (15.15)	113 (51.83)	41 (18.8)	19 (8.71)	8 (3.67)	4 (1.84)	218 (100.0)
Karnataka	21 (9.56)	8 (3.63)	60 (27.27)	108 (49.09)	12 (5.45)	11 (5.0)	220 (100.0)
Total	54 (0.12)	121 (0.28)	101 (0.23)	127 (0.29)	20 (0.05)	15 (0.03)	438 (100.0)

(*Note* : Figures in brackets show percentage)

In the study, the research team tried to explore the type of family of the respondents. In Uttar Pradesh 64.22 per cent had joint family and 35.78 per cent enjoy nuclear family (table – 5.09). Karnataka represents different picture that there is 75.91 per cent are from nuclear family. Thus, there is no specific causal factor to become destitute because here joint and nuclear family both are responsible.

J. Family Occupation of Respondents

Generally, occupation is a parameter of economic empowerment in the society which scales the social status. Maslow's theory of Need of Hierarchy is very pertinent in Indian society. For the study purpose, occupation has been classified into business, self-employment, service, labour, agriculture and others. Maximum numbers are occupied by labour occupation in Uttar Pradesh (table – 5.10). During the field study, it was found that one-fourth women are from the labour community. Similarly in Karnataka, there are 54.55 per cent women from same labour profession. It shows that due to poverty and no permanent employment, they have to suffer a lot and ultimately they try to approach shelter home for their basic need and security.

K. Annual Family Income of Respondents

Economic poverty is also one causal factor for destitute. This is revealed in table – 5.11. Women in Uttar Pradesh have maximum number of earning slab upto 2000 and this is 51.83 per cent of the total sample. Though, there are 3.67 per cent and 1.84 per cent destitute women where family income ranges between 8000 to 11000 and 11000 and above respectively. While 49.09 per cent women in Karnataka have the family income between 5000 to 8000 which is approximately half of the total sample (Table – 5.11).

6

Facilities Available at Swadhar Homes

A. Awareness of Women Development Programmes/ Schemes

In field study, an endeavour was made to know about Women Development Programmes from the home residents. Awareness about the programme is completely negligible in context of Uttar Pradesh. Only 3.66 per cent acknowledged that they are aware of the programmes, rest 96.34 per cent have completely negated the response while in Karnataka, 63.63 per cent women are aware of

Table – 6.1: Awareness of Women Development Programmes/Schemes

State	*Yes*	*No*	*Total*
Uttar Pradesh	8 (3.66)	210 (96.34)	218 (100.0)
Karnataka	140 (63.63)	80 (36.37)	220 (100.0)
Total	**148 (33.79)**	**290 (66.21)**	**438 (100.0)**

(*Note* : Figures in brackets show percentage)

Table – 6.2: Source of Information Regarding Development Programmes/Schemes

State	*NGO*	*Friends*	*Relatives*	*Media*	*Govt. Officials*	*Total*
Uttar Pradesh	3 (37.5)	–	–	3 (37.5)	2 (25.0)	8 (100.0)
Karnataka	90 (64.29)	20 (14.28)	13 (9.28)	7 (5.00)	10 (7.15)	140 (100.0)
Total	93 (62.8)	20 (13.5)	13 (8.8)	10 (6.8)	12 (8.1)	148 (100.0)

(*Note* : Figures in brackets show percentage)

Table – 6.3: Mode of Approach to Home

State	*Police*	*NGO*	*Friends*	*Relatives*	*Media*	*Others*	*Total*
Uttar Pradesh	40 (18.35)	39 (17.89)	52 (23.86)	68 (31.19)	8 (3.67)	11 (5.04)	218 (100.0)
Karnataka	24 (10.9)	120 (54.55)	18 (8.18)	22 (10.0)	10 (4.56)	26 (11.81)	220 (100.0)
Total	64 (14.61)	159 (36.3)	70 (15.98)	90 (20.56)	18 (4.1)	37 (8.45)	438 (100.0)

(*Note* : Figures in brackets show percentage)

these programmes. This reflects that South Indians are more knowledgeable than North Indians which is also a significant feature of literacy level, amongst both states. Though overall 66.21 per cent women are ignorant (table – 6.1).

B. Source of Information about Development Programmes/Schemes

To assess the instrumental source for development programmes, Non-Governmental Organisations (NGOs), friends, relatives, media and Government officials were taken into consideration. As in total eight respondents of Uttar Pradesh, 37.5 per cent women are informed by Non-Government Organisations and Media respectively. Where 64.29 per cent women in Karnataka said through non-government organisations. Friends (14.28 per cent) in Karnataka also play important role for awakening women about development programmes. Thus, Karnataka people are more prone about destitute women in comparison to Uttar Pradesh.

C. Mode of Approach to Home

Investigator team was keen to know about the right path and right mode of approach for women upto shelter home. Different type of approaches are grouped through people, NGO, friends, relatives, media and others 31.19 per cent women in Uttar Pradesh are advised by their relatives. Though 5.04 per cent destitute women approached to home by others like God etc especially in Mathura. More than half of the sample *i.e.*, 54.55 per cent women in Karnataka are shown the path of Swadhar Shelter Home through NGOs. Relatives are also seen supportive to pave the path of home in Karnataka which is 10.0 per cent of the sample. Overall 36.3 per cent NGOs are more effective for destitute women to approach swadhar homes.

D. Problems in Approaching Home

The destitute women were asked whether they faced any problem in approaching home. 86.23 per cent of Uttar Pradesh destitute women explained that they faced no problem while 13.77 per cent women confessed that they faced some problems in approaching home. As compared to UP, 50.09 per cent women in Karnataka faced different challenges while approaching homes (table – 6.4).

Table – 6.4: Problems in Approaching Home

State	*Yes*	*No*	*Total*
Uttar Pradesh	30 (13.77)	188 (86.23)	**218** **(100.0)**
Karnataka	130 (50.09)	90 (49.91)	**220** **(100.0)**
Total	**160** **(36.53)**	**278** **(63.47)**	438 (100.0)

(*Note:* Figures in brackets show percentage)

E. Types of Problems

In man-dominating society, every individual is not necessary to be honest, loyal, helpful, trust worthy etc. Apart from it, ignorance is also a great cause to create the problem. In Uttar Pradesh, 70 per cent women faced such type of problems. Whereas 92.3 per cent destitute women

Table – 6.5: Type of Problems

State	*Lack of Information*	*Role of Middlemen*	*Total*
Uttar Pradesh	21 (70.0)	9 (30.0)	30 (100.0)
Karnataka	120 (92.3)	10 (7.7)	130 (100.0)
Total	**141** **(88.1)**	**19** **(11.9)**	**160** **(100.0)**

(*Note:* Figures in brackets show percentage)

Table – 6.6: Factors for Staying in Home

State	*Eco. Crisis*	*Family Dispute*	*Desti–tution*	*Safe Secure Place*	*Better Facilities*	*Refer. By Police*	*Refer. by Court*	*Others*	*Total*
Uttar Pradesh	109 (50.0)	19 (8.7)	18 (8.3)	11 (5.0)	20 (9.1)	15 (6.9)	18 (8.3)	8 (3.7)	218 (100.0)
Karnataka	112 (50.9)	20 (9.1)	4 (1.8)	12 (5.4)	21 (9.6)	39 (17.7)	9 (4.1)	3 (1.4)	220 (100.0)
Total	**221** **(50.4)**	**39** **(8.9)**	**22** **(5.0)**	**23** **(5.3)**	**41** **(9.4)**	**54** **(2.3)**	**27** **(6.2)**	**11** **(2.5)**	**438** **(100.0)**

(*Note* : Figures in brackets show percentage)

in Karnataka revealed lack of information. In some cases, they were misguided too by the middlemen. Mostly women do not have proper knowledge and due to ignorance they fail to access where about of home.

F. Factors for Staying in Home

Reaction takes place after action in human behaviour too. In Indian society, females are known as goddess. But irony and destiny runs faster. Research team tried to know that what are the reasons which compelled destitute women to reach to home. To analyse the factors, all responses were classified into several section *i.e.*, economic crisis, family dispute, destitution, safe and secure place, better facilities, referred by police, by court and others. 50.0 per cent and 50.9 per cent women made responsible to economic crisis of Uttar Pradesh and Karnataka respectively. It reflects that poverty is the main cause which does not fulfill their basic needs. Due to family dispute 8.7 per cent women of Uttar Pradesh are staying in homes, while 9.1 per cent women in Karnataka which is marginal high as that of Uttar Pradesh. Sample exposed to family dispute. Destitute is also one reason amongst all the factors which motivate them. 8.3 per cent Uttar Pradesh women are due to destitute where 1.8 per cent women of Karnataka in comparison to Uttar Pradesh. Though five per cent and 5.4 per cent women of Uttar Pradesh and Karnataka felt home as safe and secure place. They feel insecure in family and elsewhere. 9.1 per cent and 9.6 per cent women of Uttar Pradesh and Karnataka sample replied for better facilities. Thus, half of the total samples fonds due to economic crisis. Table – 6.6 reveals that think tank of women in India have the same attitude, horizon, feelings irrespective of their native land.

G. Duration of Stay

To make a critical analysis, stay tenure in home is also a very valuable variable. Duration of stay in home is asked to the respondent women. For the above purpose, six types

Table – 6.7: Duration of Stay at Home

State	*<3 Months*	*3–6 Months*	*6–9 Months*	*9–12 Months*	*12–18 Months*	*>18 Months*	*Total*
Uttar Pradesh	22 (10.1)	11 (5.0)	19 (8.7)	11 (5.0)	19 (8.7)	136 (62.5)	218 (100.0)
Karnataka	12 (5.5)	55 (25.0)	44 (20.0)	28 (12.7)	64 (29.1)	17 (7.7)	220 (100.0)
Total	34 (7.8)	66 (15.1)	63 (14.4)	39 (8.9)	83 (18.9)	153 (34.9)	438 (100.0)

(*Note*: Figures in brackets show percentage)

of parameters are being applied to this variable *i.e.* less than three months, three – six months, six – nine months, nine – 12 months, 12–18 months and more than 18 months. In Uttar Pradesh, 62.5 per cent women stay more than 18 months long period whereas 29.1 per cent women in Karnataka are residing between 12 – 18 months duration. Just double of Karnataka respondents 10.1 per cent women are new comers *i.e.* less than three months. In total 34.9 per cent women are staying in home for more than 18 months.

H. Security Measures at Home

Security is main concern about females. Women in home feel more secured than anywhere else in the society. They feel more satisfied as data depicts in table – 6.8. In Uttar Pradesh 90.0 per cent and in Karnataka 95.5 per cent women assured that they feel more secured in homes. Very few women opined dissatisfaction.

Table – 6.8: Security Measures at Homes

State	*Satisfied*	*Dissatisfied*	*Total*
Uttar Pradesh	196 (90.0)	22 (10.0)	218 (100.0)
Karnataka	210 (95.5)	10 (4.5)	220 (100.0)
Total	**406 (92.7)**	**32 (7.3)**	**438 (100.0)**

(*Note*: Figures in brackets show percentage)

I. Availability of Medical Facilities at Homes

Homes are accountable for every walk of life. Thus, they are prone to care in terms of medical facilities. In Uttar Pradesh, 65.1 per cent respondents replied in favour of regularly medical care. While in Karnataka, cent per cent women are satisfied with the medical facilities available at homes (Table – 6.9).

Table – 6.9: Medical Facilities at Homes

State	*Regularly*	*Sometimes*	*Occasionally*	*Never*	*Total*
Uttar Pradesh	142 (65.1)	65 (29.8)	11 (5.1)	–	218 (100.0)
Karnataka	220 (100.0)	–	–	–	220 (100.0)
Total	362 (82.6)	65 (14.9)	11 (2.5)	–	438 (100.0)

(*Note* : Figures in brackets show percentage)

Table – 6.10: Provision of Four Time Meals

State	*Regularly*	*Sometimes*	*Occasionally*	*Never*	*Total*
Uttar Pradesh	139 (63.8)	19 (8.7)	60 (27.5)	–	218 (100.0)
Karnataka	148 (67.3)	11 (5.0)	61 (27.7)	–	220 (100.0)
Total	**287** **(65.5)**	**30** **(6.9)**	**121** **(27.6)**	–	**438** **(100.0)**

(*Note* : Figures in brackets show percentage)

Table – 6.11: Quality of Food

State	*Very Good*	*Good*	*Average*	*Bad*	*Total*
Uttar Pradesh	125	32	61	–	218
	(57.3)	(14.7)	(28.0)		(100.0)
Karnataka	88	120	12	–	220
	(40.0)	(54.5)	(5.5)		(100.0)
Total	213	152	73	–	438
	(48.6)	(34.7)	(16.7)		(100.0)

(*Note*: Figures in brackets show percentage)

J. Number of Meals at Homes

Home is supposed to cater four time meals to women in their respective accommodation. Mixed responses are given by inmates. 63.8 per cent destitute women in Uttar Pradesh and 67.3 per cent destitute women in Karnataka replied that they enjoy four time meals a day (table – 6.10). Only 27.5 per cent women negate that they enjoy four times meals not regularly.

K. Quality of Food

Indians are popular for their food habits. Especially, women who cook and serve different cusine to their families. Though they are by any reason prefer to reside in homes, but their taste, liking-disliking also come along theirs. On the question of quality of food, 57.3 per cent in Uttar Pradesh women gave their feedback as very good. While in Karnataka only 40 per cent respondents came in favour of very good meal. But 54.5 per cent assured that they are getting good quality of food (table – 6.11).

L. Behaviour of Home Personnel Towards Respondents

Environment is co-related with their surroundings. And in Home, surrounding means the personnel who look after them. Their attitude and behaviour is main concern for females. 62.0 per cent and 98.2 per cent destitute women are satisfied by the behaviour of home personnel in Uttar Pradesh and Karnataka

Table – 6.12: Behaviour of Home Personnel

State	*Satisfied*	*Somewhat Satisfied*	*Not Satisfied*	*Total*
Uttar Pradesh	135 (62.0)	46 (21.0)	37 (17.0)	218 (100.0)
Karnataka	216 (98.2)	2 (0.9)	2 (0.9)	220 (100.0)
Total	**351** **(80.0)**	**48** **(11.0)**	**39** **(9.0)**	**438** **(100.0)**

(*Note* : Figures in brackets show percentage)

respectively. 21.0 per cent of Uttar Pradesh respondents are somewhat satisfied by the behaviour of home people. Might be it does not match with their feelings. In total 80.0 per cent respondents presented their satisfaction level in this regard (table – 6.12).

M. Visit of Family Members

Family members of Home women have no bondings with them. A large number of family members do not or never visit home (table – 6.13). In both states, more or less same percentage of women responded *i.e.,* 73.9 per cent in Uttar Pradesh and 82.7 per cent in Karnataka responded that their family members never visit home.

N. Moving Back to Family

In Uttar Pradesh, 77.5 per cent women do not want to go back to their family while 22.5 per cent women have no idea and confused. But so far Karnataka is concerned; they are keen to go back to home *i.e.* 91.4 per cent women responded in this favour. Women in Uttar Pradesh are completely vanished infatuation towards family. They still feel anger and try to get rid of past memories and trying to enjoy the present (table – 6.14). Karnataka women are keen to go back to family where their past stay at their family dominates over the present scenario so they have faith in going back to their family. Thus, women in Uttar Pradesh are strict and tough in taking a decision about their movement back to the family.

O. Acceptance by Family and Society

Prismatic society is main feature of third world country. Families are orthodox in nature and have rigid thought process. Here people have more interest in others family matter that what happened and what is their next move etc which is conventional in nature. While diffracted society is completely different from the above one. 77.5 per cent women of Uttar Pradesh perceive that their family and society will not accept them after coming back. They have apprehension for not acceptance. But 65.9 per cent women in Karnataka assured

Table – 6.13: Visit of Family Members at Homes

State	*Regularly*	*Sometimes*	*Occasionally*	*Never*	*Total*
Uttar Pradesh	8 (3.7)	19 (8.6)	30 (13.8)	161 (73.9)	218 (100.0)
Karnataka	12 (5.5)	10 (4.5)	16 (7.3)	182 (82.7)	220 (100.0)
Total	20 (4.6)	29 (6.6)	46 (10.5)	343 (78.3)	438 (100.0)

(*Note* : Figures in brackets show percentage)

Table – 6.14: Moving Back to the Family

State	*Yes*	*No*	*No Response*	*Total*
Uttar Pradesh	–	169 (77.5)	49 (22.5)	218 (100.0)
Karnataka	201 (91.4)	19 (8.6)	–	220 (100.0)
Total	201 (45.9)	188 (42.9)	49 (11.2)	438 (100.0)

(*Note* : Figures in brackets show percentage)

Table – 6.15: Acceptance by Family and Society

State	*Yes*	*No*	*Can't Say*	*Total*
Uttar Pradesh	–	169 (77.5)	49 (22.5)	218 (100.0)
Karnataka	145 (65.9)	50 (22.7)	25 (11.4)	220 (100.0)
Total	145 (33.0)	219 (50.0)	74 (16.9)	438 (100.0)

(*Note* : Figures in brackets show percentage)

that their family and society will accept them after coming back and forgive the past circumstances (table – 6.15).

Table – 6.16: Age-wise Awareness of Development Programme

Age	*UP*		*Karnataka*	
Group	*Aware*	*Not Aware*	*Aware*	*Not Aware*
< 20	–	–	20	14
21 – 30	–	–	68	37
31 – 40	–	4	34	29
41 – 50	4	13	18	–
51 – 60	4	61	–	–
60 +	–	132	–	–
Total	**8**	**210**	**140**	**80**

In Uttar Pradesh, total eight respondents are seen who have acknowledged about the awareness of development programmes. These respondents belong to age groups between 41–50 and 51–60 years respectively. Thus, both age groups share fifty–fifty per cent of the total sample. If we take the sample of Karnataka, the data shows reverse trend. 48.6 per cent respondents are from the age group 21–30. Thus, it is very clear from the data that there is a significant difference in mind-set and attitude in terms of development between both the states. Good habits constitute the social system which is completely lacking in the state of Uttar Pradesh.

Table – 6.17 depicts the co–relation between age group and problems faced in approaching home. A very little 13.3 per cent respondents of age group 31–40 faced problems in approaching home whole women more than 60 years of age which constitute 70 per cent also faced difficulty to reach home. It shows that older women got a tough task in approaching home as compared to younger one. But in case of Karnataka, the situation is

Table – 6.17: Age-wise Problems in Approaching Home

Age Group	*UP*		*Karnataka*	
	Yes	*No*	*Yes*	*No*
< 20	–	–	20	14
21 – 30	–	–	70	35
31 – 40	4	–	25	38
41 – 50	–	17	15	3
51 – 60	5	60	–	–
60 +	21	111	–	–
Total	**30**	**188**	**130**	**90**

different because 53.8 per cent of 21-30 age group opined more problems than women of other groups. So, the life experience and span play an important role to understand the behaviour and culture of the society. Young women can be easily misguided and infatuated then aged one which is clearly seen in case of Karnataka.

An attempt has also been made to develop relationship between age and factors for staying in shelter homes. In Uttar Pradesh, 59.9 per cent women of more than sixty years age like to stay in shelter homes due to economic crisis. To resolve the pathetic condition, they prefer to stay in shelter homes, while 83.3 per cent and 66.7 per cent of same age group women resides in home following the order of court or referred by police respectively. Family dispute is also causal factor but in UP, it is not much impressive. More representation is seen between 50 to 60 and above age group women.

In Karnataka, 62.5 per cent women belong to the age group of 21–30 who are staying in shelter homes because of economic crisis which is more significant and impressive than Uttar Pradesh where economic factor was shown by upper age group.

Table – 6.18: Age-wise Factors for Staying in Home in Uttar Pradesh

Factors	*Age Groups*						*Total*
	<20	*21 – 30*	*31 – 40*	*41 – 50*	*51 – 60*	*60 +*	
Economic Crisis	–	–	2	12	30	65	109
Family Dispute	–	–	2	5	5	7	19
Desti–tution	–	–	–	–	9	9	18
Safe and Secure Place	–	–	–	–	4	7	11
Better Facilities	–	–	–	–	9	11	20
Referred by Police	–	–	–	–	5	10	15
Referred by Court	–	–	–	–	3	15	18
Others	–	–	–	–	–	8	8
Total	–	–	4	17	65	132	218

Table – 6.19: Age-wise Factors for Staying in Home in Karnataka

Factors	*Age Groups*						*Total*
	< 20	*21 – 30*	*31 – 40*	*41 – 50*	*51 – 60*	*60 +*	
Economic Crisis	10	70	25	7	–	–	112
Family Dispute	8	4	4	4	–	–	20
Desti–tution	2	2	–	–	–	–	4
Safe and Secure Place	4	7	1	–	–	–	12
Better Facilities	9	6	6	–	–	–	21
Referred by Police	1	6	25	7	–	–	39
Referred by Court	–	7	2	–	–	–	9
Others	–	3	–	–	–	–	3
Total	34	105	63	18	–	–	220

Table – 6.20: Marital Status-wise Mode of Approaching to Home in Uttar Pradesh

Factors	*Age Groups*						*Total*
	< 20	*21 – 30*	*31 – 40*	*41 – 50*	*51 – 60*	*60 +*	
Economic Crisis	10	70	25	7	–	–	112
Family Dispute	8	4	4	4	–	–	20
Desti–tution	2	2	–	–	–	–	4
Safe and Secure Place	4	7	1	–	–	–	12
Better Facilities	9	6	6	–	–	–	21
Referred by Police	1	6	25	7	–	–	39
Referred by Court	–	7	2	–	–	–	9
Others	–	3	–	–	–	–	3
Total	34	105	63	18	–	–	220

Safety and security of early age in women is a matter of great concern. This was also opined by 33.3 per cent and 58.3 per cent women of age group below twenty and upper thirty years. More than half of the total sample *i.e.* 50.9 per cent women preferred the shelter homes stay due to economic crisis. Maximum number of destitute women belongs to the age group of 21–30 years. Overall 47.7 per cent women are representing this age group of the total sample.

During the field study, a question was asked to beneficiaries by which mode you reached home. In table – 6.20, the researcher tried to develop relationship between marital status and mode of approaching home. In Uttar Pradesh, 25 per cent married women as well as 60 per cent widow were sent to home with the help of police. Major role was played by relatives and friends, who constitute 31.2 and 23.9 per cent of the total sample respectively. Here widow represents the maximum number of living in home. 87.1 per cent, 92.3 per cent, 97 per cent and 75 per cent widows were helped by NGO, friends, relatives and media respectively for approaching to shelter homes. The sample data represents that in more than 30 per cent cases, relatives played a vital role in sending home. It reflects the mind-set of the society. A mother who sincerely cares whole life for children sister always ties the knot of Rakhi to brother for his well being, wife resembles her husband as Parmeshwar (god), means male part of the society is always being cared by women where men do not have any emotions, feelings for the miserable condition of women.

So far in Karnataka, NGOs are more helpful (54.6 per cent) in guiding married women to shelter homes. Police and others have same percentage in showing path of home to married women. 41.6 per cent and 39.2 per cent unmarried women have opined that they got helping hand of police and NGO respectively. In comparison to Uttar Pradesh, here married women represent maximum number. It shows that the married couples do not have faith to lead happy married life in longer terms.

Table – 6.21: Marital Status-wise Mode of Approaching Home in Karnataka

Marital Status	*Mode of Approach to Home*						*Total*
	Police	*NGO*	*Friends*	*Relatives*	*Media*	*Others*	
Married	12	52	6	11	4	12	97
Unmarried	10	47	2	4	2	3	68
Divorcee	1	5	3	2	1	–	12
Widow	1	15	3	3	3	2	27
Separated	–	1	4	2	–	9	16
Total	24	120	18	22	10	26	220

Table – 6.22: Occupation-wise Factors for Staying in Home in Uttar Pradesh

Factors	*Occupation*				*Total*
	Domestic Service	*Labour*	*Private Service*	*Others*	
Economic Crisis	15	45	18	31	109
Family Dispute	5	5	4	5	19
Desti–tution	7	5	3	3	18
Safe and Secure Place	3	5	2	1	11
Better Facilities	2	7	6	5	20
Referred by Police	2	6	4	3	15
Referred by Court	2	8	1	7	18
Others	1	2	2	3	8
Total	37	83	40	58	218

Table – 6.22 depicts correlation between occupation and causing factors which compelled women to stay in shelter homes in Uttar Pradesh. 40.6 per cent women of domestic services are staying in home due to the economic crisis. 54.2 per cent women in labour community stay in home for economic reasons. Though 50 per cent women of total sample show financial causes for staying in home. Among this category, maximum number *i.e.*, 41.3 per cent women belongs to labour category. Women of every occupation represent more or less same percentage due to family disputes. 38.9 per cent women of domestic services are staying in home due to destitution. While 45.5 per cent labour community women prefer to remain in home for safety and security reasons. It means women in labour sector have very poor and sad experience against men in the society by their nature and behaviour. Again, 35 per cent of women in labour class opined their views that they want to remain in home for the sake of better facilities. Lack of infrastructural facilities in society obstacle to cater basic essential needs for their survival. 45.5 per cent and 44.4 per cent destitute women of labour occupation were referred by police and court respectively. Women in Uttar Pradesh of labour occupation are vulnerable. Data reveals that maximum number of labour community destitute women stay in home because of different factors.

In Karnataka, 50.9 per cent destitute women stay in home due to economic crisis irrespective of their occupation. Women of domestic service and private service represent the same percentage *i.e.* 14.5 per cent each. Women in labour occupation are slightly higher than the women engaged in other work which is 19.1 per cent amongst all factors. 31.3 per cent and 37.6 per cent women belonging to domestic service profession stay in home due to the paucity of fund or financially weak and police reference respectively. Thus, in both the sampled states, more representation is seen by the women belonging to labour class. Though in Uttar Pradesh the percentage of destitute women is double than in Karnataka. 37.6 per cent women of private

Table – 6.23: Occupation-wise Factors for Staying in Home in Karnataka

Factors	*Occupation*				*Total*
	Domestic Service	*Labour*	*Private Service*	*Others*	
Economic Crisis	10	14	12	76	112
Family Dispute	2	4	4	10	20
Destitution	1	1	2	–	4
Safe and Secure Place	2	4	2	4	12
Better Facilities	3	3	5	10	21
Referred by Police	12	9	5	13	39
Referred by Court	2	4	2	1	9
Others	–	3	–	–	3
Total	32	42	32	114	220

Table – 6.24: Ecological Background-wise Factors for Staying in Home

Factors	*Uttar Pradesh*			*Karnataka*		
	Urban	*Semi-Urban*	*Rural*	*Urban*	*Semi-Urban*	*Rural*
Economic Crisis	30	65	14	35	12	65
Family Dispute	4	11	4	5	4	11
Destitution	4	10	4	1	1	2
Safe and Secure Place	2	7	2	2	2	8
Better Facilities	4	12	4	3	2	16
Referred by Police	3	10	2	19	5	15
Referred by Court	11	7	–	2	2	5
Others	2	3	3	1	–	2
Total	60	125	33	68	28	124

service occupation opined to remain in shelter home because of fiscal problems. Poverty which is defined in terms of per capita income in the third world countries is main causal factor. At least in home, their satisfaction level is higher than outside.

The scholar made an endeavour to develop relationship between factors staying in home and ecological background. In Uttar Pradesh, 52 per cent women belonging to semi-urban areas have shown the cause of economic crisis which is the maximum in number. While in Karnataka, 52.4 per cent women from rural areas are staying in home for the reason of economic crisis. In family dispute factor, 12.1 per cent women from rural background of Uttar Pradesh are staying in home. But in Karnataka, 14.3 per cent women from semi-urban background are staying in home due to family disputes. For safety factors, both state represents more or less equal percentage from rural areas. Better facilities are also deep concern for women from rural background in Uttar Pradesh and Karnataka which is 12.2 per cent and 12.9 per cent respectively. The role of police is more prominent in Karnataka where 27.9 per cent of women from urban areas are referred to home. In democracy, third pillar is known as judiciary apart from legislative and executive. 18.3 per cent women of Uttar Pradesh of urban localities were referred by court. Overall, 57.3 per cent semi-urban and 56.4 per cent rural females stay in home. It reveals that destitution is more rampant in rural areas of Karnataka than Uttar Pradesh.

Diversity of culture, religion, languages etc. is known as 'INDIA'. Though this the study is comparative, based between two different states, one from North and other from South. Table No. – 6.25 depicts relationship of religion and causal factors affecting women for staying in home. In Northern region, Uttar Pradesh, the women staying in home belonged to Hindu religion and no other caste was seen in the sample. Amongst Hindu religion, 50 per cent women stay in home due to economic crisis which is half of the total sample. While in Karnataka, the women of Hindu, Muslim and Christian religion are staying

Table – 6.25: Religion-wise Factors for Staying in Home

Factors	*Uttar Pradesh*			*Karnataka*		
	Hindu	*Muslim*	*Christian*	*Hindu*	*Muslim*	*Christian*
Economic Crisis	109	–	–	102	4	6
Family Dispute	19	–	–	7	7	6
Destitution	18	–	–	4	–	–
Safe and Secure Place	11	–	–	12	–	–
Better Facilities	20	–	–	16	–	5
Referred by Police	15	–	–	39	–	–
Referred by Court	18	–	–	9		–
Others	8	–	–	1	1	1
Total	218	–	–	190	12	18

in home. Economic factor compels Hindu women (53.7 per cent) to stay in home. Other two religions share equal percentage (33.3 per cent) of each of the total sample.

7

Epilogue: Problems and Suggestions

"Discarded by families and wandering further and further away from home, women real selves are lost or submerged under layers of dirt and idiosyncrasies. They become non-persons, consciously ignored or worse, paid unhealthy attention. Women are particularly prone to be easy targets of sexual abuse. The destitute comprises a largely forgotten and unthought of section of the homeless. Lacking protection by law, there are no government plans or programmes for these people, who by law simply do not exist" (out of mind, out of sight: 2002). Present study has demonstrated the impact of social circumstances upon women's private experiences and actions. Whether it is denial of economic resources, education, legal and health services, deprivation, lack of physical and mental nurturance, exhaustation from overwork or sexual and other forms of physical and mental abuses across the life span. This corroborates that it is women who are at the great risk. These issues not only fall within the fabric of human rights but also are those which understandably affect mental health. In addition, the routine of women's lives render them at risk to experience more stress than men. This reflects the greater number of social roles women fulfill as wife, mother, daughter, care-giver and an employee. Furthermore, women's reproductive role as bearer and nurturer of children produces unique potential for stress-related effects. Indian women have witnessed a decline in their socio-economic standing against their male counterparts, according to annual Master Card World Wide Index of Women's advancement. From older times, women act as servile workers and do not take part in decision-making.

The detailed analysis of the various aspects of the study are dealt in earlier portion of the report. Here, we present only major problems which have emerged out of the study as follows:

1. People come along with their habits. It is visible in home, that women behave in different manner with each other. Some of them pollute the whole environment of home due to quarrelling with other women.
2. They are seen very depressed.
3. Their confidence level seems to be very low.
4. Their lonely struggle for survival makes them vulnerable to sexual abuse and other kind of exploitations.
5. Onus of poverty is shared only by them.
6. They are known as deprived class and second class citizens in family as well as in society.
7. They are given less rights and privileges.
8. More women than men are said to suffer from mental disorders.
9. They never share their problems with home officials.
10. Nuclear family culture is also the main cause.

Administrative Problems of Home

To smoothly manage and govern any organisation, there are three main components *viz.*, men, money and material (3-M).

1. Allocated budget is not released in time.
2. Hierarchy of the organisation causes delay in performance.
3. There is no head of electricity and maintenance in the budget.
4. No one found in the post of sweeper.
5. Rent of home is not being paid timely due to delay in grant.
6. Employees of home are not getting salaries regularly.
7. There is no revision of budget since last ten years while prices of items required to fulfill day to day needs are revised frequently.
8. There is no budgetary provision for training of rehabilitation.
9. No provision for conveyance allowance.
10. There is no provision of ambulance for serious illness or in case of emergency.

Suggestions

On the basis of the findings, problems in the present study, we try to offer important suggestions which may be incorporated as the policy measures for achieving desired goals and strengthening women livelihood as follows:

1. To make legislation is not remedial measure to sort out problems, unless is not implemented and executed properly and honestly.

2. Counsellors should take more pain in counselling families and their destitute women.
3. Counsellors should apprise fairly to the families of women about their respective problems and try to mitigate those annoyances.
4. More social workers and NGOs should come forward and try to mediate in solving the problems.
5. State Commission for Women should be made more active vis–a–vis mentally ill women.
6. It should act as monitoring authority for state run institutions so that human rights violation can be checked.
7. Encouragement to be given to self-help groups.
8. Short-term training programmes, specialised courses should be encouraged for their stand in society after coming back from shelter homes.
9. A comprehensive "Rehabilitation Policy" should be evolved by the government to help in integration of destitute women back in society.
10. For fooding, allocation of fund is Rs 500 only which is a meagre amount and insufficient to cater the basic need of a person. Amount should be Rs 1500/– per head.
11. The present allocated release fund is for inmates of home and rented building is Rs 17500/– for 100 inmates. It needs enhancement in fund at the present market rate.
12. Joint family culture should be promoted and inculcated because it has a lot of merits as compared to demerits.

INTERVIEW SCHEDULE FOR WOMEN BENEFICIARIES

Appendices

Empowerment of Destitute Women: A Comparative Study of Swadhar Shelter Homes in Uttar Pradesh and Karnataka

Sponsored by
Indian Council of Social Science Research, New Delhi

Conducted by
Institute for Applied Research and Development, Lucknow

1. General Information

1.1 State:

1.2 District :

1.3 City:

1.4 Name of Institution/ Organisation:

1.5 Name of Swadhar Shelter Home:

1.6 Name of Respondent:

2. Respondent's Profile

2.1 Age of Respondent:

1. Less than 20 years

2. 20–30 years
3. 30–40 years
4. 40–50 years
5. 50–60 years
6. Above 60 years

2.2 Marital Status:

1. Married
2. Unmarried
3. Divorced
4. Widow
5. Separated

2.3 Educational Background:

1. Illiterate
2. Literate
3. Primary
4. Jr. High School
5. High School
6. Intermediate
7. Graduate
8. Others (Specify)

2.4 Occupation of Respondent :

1. Domestic Service
2. Labour
3. Private Service

4. Other (Specify)

2.5 Whether your parents/close relatives are alive

1. Yes ☐ 2. No ☐

3.0 Family Background

3.1 Ecological Background

1. Urban ☐
2. Semi-urban ☐
3. Rural ☐

3.2 Religion

1. Hindu ☐
2. Muslim ☐
3. Christian ☐
4. Sikh ☐
5. Jain ☐
6. Buddhist ☐
7. Others ☐

3.3 Caste

1. General ☐ 2. OBC ☐ 3. SC ☐
4. ST ☐ 5. Others ☐

3.4 Type of Family

1. Joint ☐ 2. Nuclear ☐

3.5 Family Occupation

1. Pety Business ☐
2. Self-employment ☐
3. Service ☐

4. Labour ☐
5. Agriculture ☐
6. Non–farm Sector ☐
7. Others

3.6 Annual Family Income from all Sources

4. Awareness Regarding Social Development Programmes/ Schemes

4.1 Are you aware about the social development programmes/schemes being funded by the Government and legislations?

1. Yes ☐ 2. No ☐

4.2 What are the main source of information regarding these schemes/programmes and legislations?

1. Workers/ Representatives of NGO ☐
2. Friends ☐
3. Relatives ☐
4. Media ☐
5. Government Officials ☐
6. Others

4.3 How do you approach to Swadhar Shelter Home?

1. Through Police ☐
2. Representative of NGO ☐
3. Recommendation of Friends ☐
4. Recommendation of Relatives ☐
5. Self -motivated through media ☐
6. Others

4.4 Whether you faced any problem in approaching Swadhar Shelter Home?

1. Yes ☐ 2. No ☐

If Yes :

a. Lack of Information ☐

b. Wastage of Time ☐

c. Role of Middle man ☐

d. Many frequent visits to home for admission ☐

e. Others

5. Reasons for Staying in Home

5.1 What are the main reasons for coming and staying in home?

1. Economic Crisis ☐
2. Family Dispute ☐
3. Destitution ☐
4. Search of Safe and Secure Place ☐
5. Intention of Better Facilities ☐
6. Rescued by Police and referred to Home ☐
7. Referred by Court ☐
8. Others

5.2 What is the duration of your stay in Home?

1. Less than three months ☐

2. 3–6 months ☐

3. 6–9 months ☐

4. 9–12 months ☐

5. 12–18 months ☐

6. More than 18 months ☐

6. Living Conditions and Availing of Services

6.1 Are you satisfied with security measures at home?

1. Yes ☐

2. No ☐

If No Give Reasons ....

6.2 Whether medical facilities are available in Home?

1. Regularly ☐ 2. Sometimes ☐

3. Occasionally ☐ 4. Never ☐

6.3 Do you get four times meal?

1. Regularly ☐ 2. Sometimes ☐

3. Occasionally ☐ 4. Never ☐

6.4 How do you rate quality of food?

1. Very good ☐ 2. Good ☐

3. Average ☐ 4. Bad ☐

6.5 Are you satisfied with the attitude and behaviour of staff at home?

1. Satisfied ☐

2. Somewhat Satisfied ☐

3. Not Satisfied ☐

4. Can't Say ☐

6.6 Whether your family members visit you at shelter home ?

1. Regularly ☐ 2. Sometimes ☐

3. Occasionally ☐ 4. Never ☐

6.7 Given an opportunity, would you like to go back to your family ?

1. Yes ☐ 2. No ☐

6.8 Do you think that your family and society will accept you ?

1. Yes ☐ 2. No ☐

3. Can't say ☐

7. Your valuable suggestions for your rehabilitation

INTERVIEW SCHEDULE FOR SHELTER HOME

Empowerment of Destitute Women: A Comparative Study of Swadhar Shelter Homes in Uttar Pradesh and Karnataka

Sponsored by

Indian Council of Social Science Research, New Delhi

Conducted by

Institute for Applied Research and Development, Lucknow

1. General Information

1.1 State:

1.2 City:

1.3 Name of Creche Centre:

2. Infrastructure

2.1 Type of Building

1. Pucca ☐
2. Semi–Pucca ☐
3. Others

2.2 Type of Floor

1. Marble ☐ 2. Cemented ☐

3. Tiles ☐ 4. Others

2.3 Total area used for Swadhar Home (in sq. feet)

2.4 Number of Rooms in home:

2.5 Staff member present in the Swadhar home

1. Male
2. Female
3. Total

2.6 Details of women present in Home

1. No. of women inmates :
2. No. of dependent children:

3.0 Facilities

3.1 Does the home has proper and adequate following facilities ?

1. Electricity Supply Yes ☐ No ☐
2. Clean Toilets and Sanitation
   Yes ☐ No ☐
3. Clean and Safe Drinking Water
   Yes ☐ No ☐
4. Ventilation Yes ☐ No ☐
5. Play Ground and Equipment
   Yes ☐ No ☐
6. Mattress Yes ☐ No ☐
7. Carts/Beds Yes ☐ No ☐
8. Blankets/ Quilts Yes ☐ No ☐
9. Reading and Learning Materials
   Yes ☐ No ☐

10. Separate Kitchen Yes ☐ No ☐

11. Stove, Gas, Cylinders Yes ☐ No ☐

12. Cooking Utensils Yes ☐ No ☐

3.2 Medical Facilities available in Home or its adjoining areas Yes ☐ No ☐

4.0 Food and Other Essentials

4.1 Whether the home has first–aid kit,
Yes ☐ No ☐

4.2 Whether first aid kit contains the required equipment and medicines all the time,

Yes ☐ No ☐

4.3 Whether the home has facility of proper and regular chlorination or boiling of drinking water,
Yes ☐ No ☐

4.4 Whether the food is acceptable to women and children in the home, Yes ☐ No ☐

4.5 Whether the present food preparation is suitable for :

1. Maintaining nutritional value ☐

2. Cleanliness ☐

3. Taste ☐

5.0 Maintaining of Records

5.1 Maintaining and Upkeeping of records

1. Attendance Register ☐

2. Stock Register ☐

3. Other ☐

INTERVIEW SCHEDULE FOR IMPLEMENTING AGENCY

Empowerment of Destitute Women : A Comparative Study of Swadhar Shelter Homes in Uttar Pradesh and Karnataka

Sponsored by
Indian Council of Social Science Research, New Delhi

Conducted by
Institute for Applied Research and Development, Lucknow

1.0. General Information

1.1 State:

1.2 District:

1.3 City:

1.4 Name of Institution/ Organization:

1.5 Name of Respondent :

1.6 Designation of Respondent :

2.0 Infrastructure

2.1 Year of Establishment :

2.2 Whether registered under Societies Registration Act, 1860:

1. Yes ☐ 2. No ☐

2.3 Nature of organisation:

1. Government ☐
2. NGO ☐
3. Trust ☐
4. Others

2.4 Location of Head office:

1. State Capital ☐
2. District Headquarter ☐
3. Semi-urban Area ☐
4. Rural ☐

2.5 Ownership of Building:

1. Own ☐
2. Rental ☐

2.6 Staff Position:

1. Administration and Supervision
2. Project Staff
3. Field Staff
4. Staff engaged in Creche

2.7 Details of Staff members engaged in shelter home:

1. Male
2. Female

2.8 Annual Turnover of organisation in case of NGO: Rs.

2.9 Please provide the approximate proportion of grant details:

1. International Agencies

2. Central Government
3. State Government
4. Swadhar Shelter Home
5. Other:

2.10 Whether set-up Swadhar Shelter home in the premises of organisation:

1. Yes ☐ 2. No ☐

3.0 Details of Shelter Home

3.1 Since how many years, you are running the Swadhar Shelter Home/Short Stay Home:

3.2 Please provide details of Swadhar Shelter Home:

Year	*No. of Women Inmates*	*No. of Dependent Children*	*Total Budget*	*Staff Member Engaged*
2010–11				
2009–10				
2008–09				

3.3 Whether you have imposed user charges for increasing home resources:

1. Yes ☐ 2. No ☐

3.4 Whether your Swadhar Shelter home has been inspected by the organisations/sponsoring/collaborating agencies

1. Yes ☐ 2. No ☐

If yes :

a. Department of Women and Child Development

b. Department of Social Welfare

c. District Probationary Officer

d. Others

3.5 What is the periodicity of visit to the home by the officials other than home staff of organisation

1. Daily ☐ 2. Weekly ☐
3. Fortnightly ☐ 4. Monthly ☐
5. Quarterly ☐

3.6 What is the periodicity of visit to the home by the officials of sponsoring/collaborating agencies

1. Fortnightly ☐ 2. Monthly ☐
3. Quarterly ☐ 4. Half–yearly ☐
5. Annual

3.7 What is more of induction of inmates?

a. Referred by Police ☐
b. Referred by Women and Child Development Department ☐
c. Referred by Social Welfare Department ☐
d. Through Advertisement ☐
e. Referred by other NGOs ☐
f. Referred by court ☐

3.8 What is the criteria for selection of women inmates?

1. Destitute ☐
2. Poor and from BPL Family ☐
3. Victim of Crimes ☐
4. Victim of Rape ☐

5. Victim of Disaster ☐
6. Victim of Trafficking or rescued ☐
7. Homeless ☐
8. Victims of domestic violence ☐
9. Others ☐

4. Infrastructure, Amenities and Services at Home

4.1 What is more of accommodation for inmates and their dependent children?

1. Single ☐ 2. Twin Sharing ☐

3. Dormitory ☐

4.2 Whether you provide separate rooms for women inmates and their dependent children?

1. Yes ☐ 2. No ☐

4.3 Do you provide well furnished (Bed/ Chair/ Table/ Almirah) rooms to inmates?

1. Yes ☐ 2. No ☐

4.4 Whether rooms are air-cooled equipped with electric devices (bulb/ tubelight/ fans/ cooler)

1. Yes ☐ 2. No ☐

4.5 Do you provide common recreational facilities including TV?

1. Yes ☐ 2. No ☐

4.6 Whether safe drinking water facility is available in Home?

1. Yes ☐ 2. No ☐

4.7 Do you have proper security arrangement?

1. Yes ☐ 2. No ☐

4.8 How many times you provide meals to inmates?

1. One ☐

2. Two ☐

3. Three ☐

4. Four ☐

5. Don't provide meal ☐

4.9 Have you established linkages with government hospitals/ dispensaries for providing medical aid and health checkup to inmates?

1. Yes ☐ 2. No ☐

4.10 Have you established linkages with other government departments for convergence of programmes and schemes for inmates?

1. Yes ☐ 2. No ☐

4.11 Do you organise programmes for vocational training for inmates?

1. Regularly ☐

2. Sometimes ☐

3. Occasionally ☐

4. Never

4.12 Do you provide clothing to inmates?

1. Regularly ☐

2. Sometimes ☐

3. Occasionally ☐

4. Never ☐

4.13 Have you set-up women help line?

1. Yes ☐ 2. No ☐

4.14 Whether women help-line has helped you in entry and rehabilitation of destitute women?

1. Regularly ☐
2. Sometimes ☐
3. Occasionally ☐
4. Never ☐

5.0 Rehabilitation of Women

5.1 Please give the following details for rehabilitation of destitute women:

Year	*Intake/ Enrollment*	*Rehabilitated/ Went Out*	*No. of Trained Women*	*No. of Women Provided Employment*
2010–11				
2009–10				
2008–09				

6.0 What are main problems in running of Swadhar Shelter home?

7.0 Your valuable suggestions running of Swadhar Shelter home?

Bibliography

Government of India, Department of Social Welfare, Ministry of Education and Social Welfare, *Towards Equality, Report of the Committee on the Status of Women in India*, 1974.

Annual Report, Department of Women and Child Development, Ministry of HRD, Govt. of India, New Delhi.

Government of India, Planning Commission, Five Year Plans, 1951 to 2012.

Aruna Goel, *Organisation and Structure of Women Development and Empowerment, New Delhi.*

Constitution of India, Article 14.

Constitution of India, Article 15.

Report of Beijing Declaration, 1995.

Government of India, Ministry of Women and Child Development – *A National Policy for the Empowerment of Women*, 2001.

Index